The
NYSTROM
ATLAS
of
**Our
Country's
History**

n NYSTROM
DIVISION OF HERFF JONES, INC.

ontents

Three Worlds Meet, *1400 to 1682*

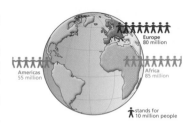

Colonial America, *1600 to 1776*

A New Nation, *1763 to 1810*

EDUCATIONAL CONSULTANTS

Dr. JoAnne Buggey, Professor, Dept. of Curriculum and Instruction, U. of Minnesota, Minneapolis, Minnesota

Betty B. Franks, Vice Chair, National Council for History Education, Maple Heights City School Dist., Maple Heights, Ohio

Dr. Jacqueline L. Frierson, Principal, IS 292 Margaret Douglas, Brooklyn, New York

Melissa Green, Classroom Teacher, Social Studies and Language Arts Depts., Evanston School Dist. #65, Evanston, Illinois

Robert Hagopian, United States History Teacher, History Dept., Scotts Valley Middle School, Scotts Valley, California

The United States Expands, *1790 to 1860*

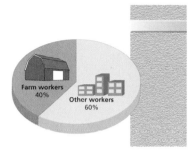

Civil War and Change, *1820 to 1900*

Modern America, *1898 to Now*

Reference Maps

PHOTO CREDITS

Credit Abbreviations
B/C Bettmann/CORBIS
C CORBIS
FPG FPG International LLC
Granger The Granger Collection, New York
NWPA North Wind Picture Archives
PQ PictureQuest
SM Stock Montage

front cover (top left) © Joseph Sohm; Visions of America/C; (top right) Granger; (bottom) © Flip Schulke/C; **back cover** © SM; **8** © SM; **10** Josef Mensing Gallery, Hamm-Rhynern, Germany/Bridgeman Art Library; **11** © Gallo Images/C; **12** © John Farmar; Cordaiy Photo Library Ltd./C; **14** © B/C; **15** © William Easton/Wood River Gallery/PQ; **17** © Peter Essick/Aurora/PQ; **19** © Sylvain Grandadam/Stone; **21** NWPA; **25** © Dorothy Littell Greco/Stock Boston Inc./PQ; **27** Granger; **29** © SuperStock, Inc.; **31** © Tim Wright/C; **32** Granger; **35** Granger; **37** © SuperStock, Inc.; **39** © Raymond Gehman/C; **40** NWPA; **43** © SM; **44** Granger; **47** NWPA; **48** © William Tyler Ranney/Wood River Gallery/PQ; **51** Granger; **52** (left) Granger; (right) Granger; **54** © B/C; **55** © FPG; **57** © B/C; **58** © SM; **59** © C; **61** © C; **63** © B/C; **64** © B/C; **65** © C; **66** © FPG; **70** AP Photo; **71** © Duomo/C; **73** © Lawrence Migdale/Stock Boston Inc./PQ.

How has our country changed over time?

The six units that begin on page 8 tell—and show—the story of our country's history. The maps on these two pages are snapshots of our country in the last year of each unit.

1682

The three worlds of Europe, Africa, and the Americas met in North America. By 1682 Europeans had claimed most of the continent as their own.

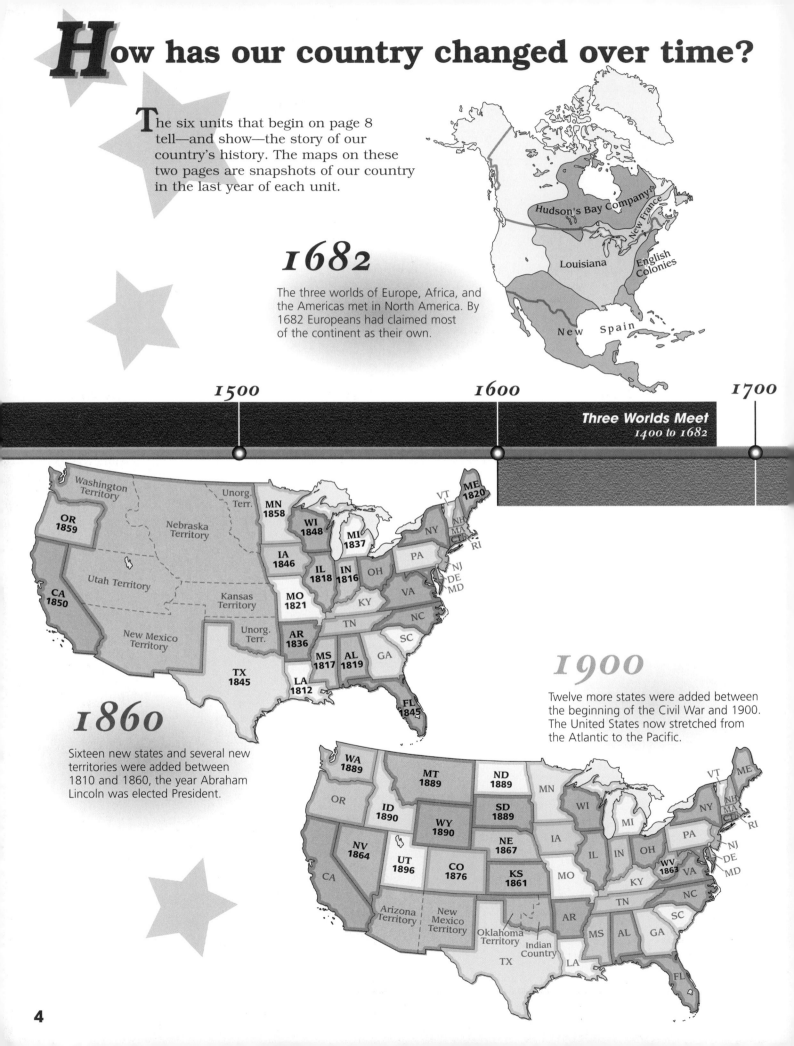

Hudson's Bay Company
New France
Louisiana
English Colonies
New Spain

1500   **1600**   **1700**

Three Worlds Meet
1400 to 1682

1860

Sixteen new states and several new territories were added between 1810 and 1860, the year Abraham Lincoln was elected President.

Washington Territory
OR 1859
CA 1850
Utah Territory
Nebraska Territory
Unorg. Terr.
New Mexico Territory
Kansas Territory
Unorg. Terr.
TX 1845
MN 1858
WI 1848
IA 1846
MO 1821
AR 1836
MS 1817
LA 1812
MI 1837
IL 1818
IN 1816
OH
KY
TN
AL 1819
GA
FL 1845
ME 1820
VT
NY
NH
MA
CT
RI
PA
NJ
DE
MD
VA
NC
SC

1900

Twelve more states were added between the beginning of the Civil War and 1900. The United States now stretched from the Atlantic to the Pacific.

WA 1889
OR
ID 1890
NV 1864
CA
UT 1896
MT 1889
WY 1890
CO 1876
Arizona Territory
New Mexico Territory
ND 1889
SD 1889
NE 1867
KS 1861
Oklahoma Territory
Indian Country
TX
MN
WI
MI
IA
MO
AR
LA
IL
IN
OH
KY
TN
MS
AL
GA
FL
WV 1863
VA
NC
SC
PA
NY
VT
ME
NH
MA
CT
RI
NJ
DE
MD

4

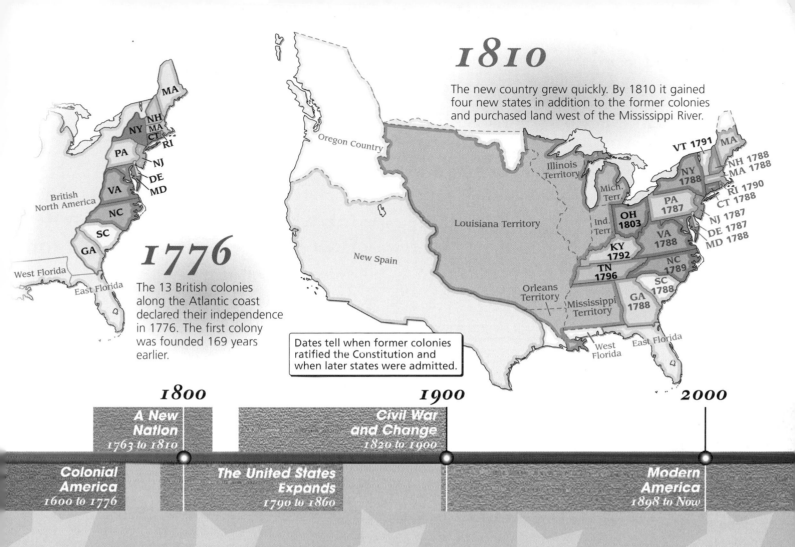

1810

The new country grew quickly. By 1810 it gained four new states in addition to the former colonies and purchased land west of the Mississippi River.

VT 1791
NY 1788
PA 1787
OH 1803
VA 1788
KY 1792
TN 1796
NC 1789
SC 1788
GA 1788

MA
NH 1788
MA 1788
RI 1790
CT 1788
NJ 1787
DE 1787
MD 1788

Oregon Country
Illinois Territory
Mich. Terr.
Louisiana Territory
Ind. Terr.
New Spain
Orleans Territory
Mississippi Territory
West Florida
East Florida

Dates tell when former colonies ratified the Constitution and when later states were admitted.

1776

The 13 British colonies along the Atlantic coast declared their independence in 1776. The first colony was founded 169 years earlier.

MA
NH
NY
MA
CT
RI
PA
NJ
DE
MD
VA
NC
SC
GA

British North America
West Florida
East Florida

1800

A New Nation
1763 to 1810

1900

Civil War and Change
1820 to 1900

2000

Colonial America
1600 to 1776

The United States Expands
1790 to 1860

Modern America
1898 to Now

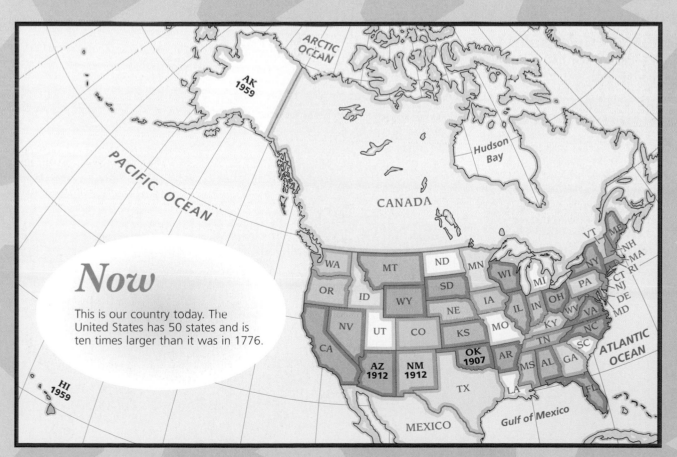

Now

This is our country today. The United States has 50 states and is ten times larger than it was in 1776.

ARCTIC OCEAN
AK 1959
PACIFIC OCEAN
Hudson Bay
CANADA
HI 1959

WA
MT
ND
MN
WI
MI
VT
ME
NH
NY
MA
CT
RI
OR
ID
WY
SD
IA
IL
IN
OH
PA
NJ
DE
MD
NV
UT
CO
NE
MO
KY
WV
VA
NC
CA
AZ 1912
NM 1912
KS
OK 1907
AR
TN
SC
MS
AL
GA
TX
LA
FL
ATLANTIC OCEAN

MEXICO
Gulf of Mexico

How does this atlas work?

This atlas tells the story of our country's history through maps, graphs, pictures, and words.

1 First read the **unit title**. The atlas is divided into six units covering six periods of U.S. history. The unit title gives the main theme of the period it covers.

2 Then read the **focus question**. The information on these two pages will help you answer it.

3 Next read the **introduction**, which will help you understand the main subject of these two pages.

4 Now follow the **A B C D** markers for the clearest path through the pages.

Maps show places, movement, people, and events from a time in our country's history.

A **map legend** gives the title of the map and explains the meanings of the colors and other symbols. Read the legend before studying the map.

Locator maps show what part of the country appears on the main map.

Some maps and graphs cover the same topics at **different times** in history. Compare them to see change over time.

The United States Expands

How did the United States grow in the mid-1800s?

In the mid-1800s, the U.S. population grew rapidly, and so did the demand for new lands.

▶ The government seized Indian lands east of the Mississippi River and then sold them to white settlers.

▶ Americans began settling in Texas, still part of Mexico. By 1836 there were so many of them there that they formed the independent Republic of Texas.

▶ The United States gained even more land after a treaty with Britain and the War with Mexico.

British	768,804
German	

Total immigrants: 4,933,9
*Includes groups not shown.

 Largest Immigrant Gr

Immigration helped our country
Compare this graph with the m
were the largest immigrant grou

Civil War and Chang

How did t in the late

After the Civil War, miner
with the protection of U.S
unsuccessfully to keep th

▶ Between 1860 and 1
lost 25 percent of th
from diseases broug
also in battles with U

▶ They also lost 90 pe
and what was left be
reservations.

▶ White hunters killed
buffalo on the Great
Indians lost their ma

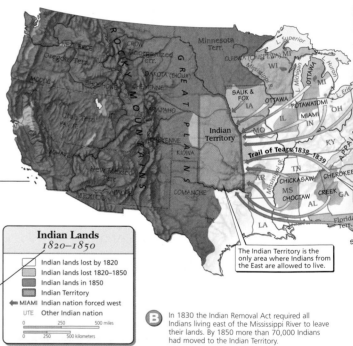

The Indian Territory is the
only area where Indians from
the East are allowed to live.

Indian Lands
1820–1850

- ☐ Indian lands lost by 1820
- Indian lands lost 1820–1850
- Indian lands in 1850
- Indian Territory
- ⬅ MIAMI Indian nation forced west
- UTE Other Indian nation

| 0 | 250 | 500 miles |
| 0 | 250 | 500 kilometers |

B In 1830 the Indian Removal Act required all Indians living east of the Mississippi River to leave their lands. By 1850 more than 70,000 Indians had moved to the Indian Territory.

46

Indian Lands
1865

CROW Indian nation
- ☐ Indian lands lost by 1865

Graphs help you compare two or more pieces of information.

Pictures show how people and places looked in the past.

C When Americans formed the Republic of Texas, thousands of Mexicans still lived there. Today roughly 3 of every 10 Texans are of Mexican descent.

Captions help you understand more about the subject of each map, graph, and picture.

1845
Texas becomes the 20th state in the United States.

Key dates describe an important event in history.

904,940

0–1860
ow quickly.
Which
imes?

American Expansion
1845–1853

How Land Was Gained

Agreement

Purchase

War

1845 Year land was gained
Map shows boundaries of today.

D In just eight years, the size of the United States grew by two-thirds. Some land was gained through war, and some by agreement or by purchase.

British North America

U.S. and Britain agree to split Oregon at 49°N.

Oregon Country
1846

Mexico loses war with U.S., gives up its northern lands.

Mexican Cession
1848

UNITED STATES
(before 1845)

ME.

NH
MA
CT
RI

DE

rced move,
okees dies.

Republic of Texas accepts offer from U.S. Congress to be added to the United States.

ATLANTIC OCEAN

Gadsden Purchase
1853

U.S. buys Mexican land for a southern railroad route.

Texas Annexation
1845

PACIFIC OCEAN

Gulf of Mexico

MEXICO

47

What else is in this atlas?

How many people live in Texas today? Check the **State Facts** on the inside front cover.

Where can you locate places in the United States and the world today? Use the **Reference Maps** on pages 74–81.

What does "treaty" mean? Find it in the **Glossary** on pages 82–83.

What does "R." stand for? Check the **Abbreviations** on pages 82–83.

Where can you find more information about Indians? Use the **Index** on pages 84–87.

Who was the president in 1846? Check the list of **Presidents of the United States** on page 88.

How big is the United States today? See **Facts About the United States** on the inside back cover.

1870
Dakota and Cheyenne warriors overwhelm U.S. troops at the Battle of Little Bighorn, also known as Custer's Last Stand.

90 many Indian children were being sent to boarding schools. they had to give up traditional Indian names and ways of life.

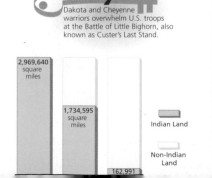

2,969,640
square
miles

1,734,595
square
miles

Indian Land

Non-Indian Land

162,991

Who were the first Americans?

The worlds of Europe, Africa, and America did not meet until after 1492. The people who lived in the Americas before then are known as Native Americans, or *Indians*.

▶ At the time of Columbus's first voyage, there were more than 500 Indian nations.

▶ Most Indians lived in Mexico or farther south. But millions lived in what is now Canada and the United States.

▶ Indian nations developed a variety of tools, shelters, languages, and religions.

▶ Some Indians were *nomadic*, moving from place to place. But most lived in permanent settlements.

A Many Native Americans lived in small villages. They built their shelters, hunted or grew their food, and made their own tools and clothing.

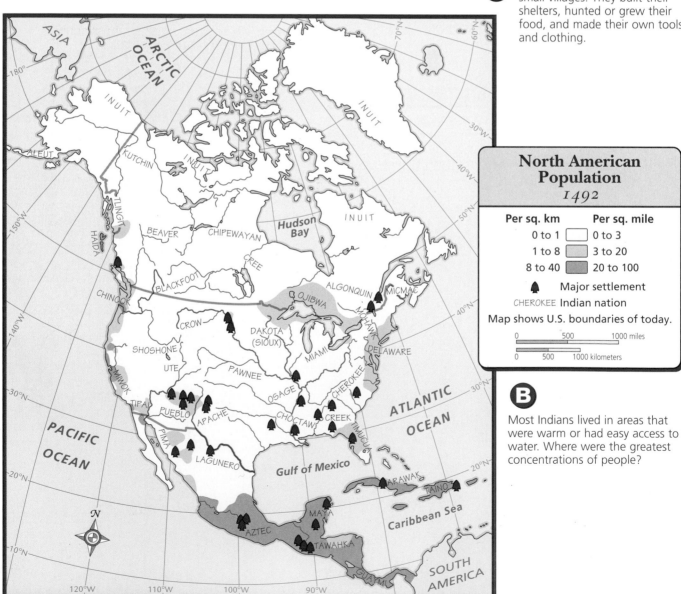

North American Population
1492

Per sq. km		Per sq. mile
0 to 1		0 to 3
1 to 8		3 to 20
8 to 40		20 to 100

🌲 Major settlement

CHEROKEE Indian nation

Map shows U.S. boundaries of today.

B Most Indians lived in areas that were warm or had easy access to water. Where were the greatest concentrations of people?

Typical Foods of Native Americans

	Northwest Coast	California-Intermountain	Southwest	Middle America	Plains	Eastern Woodlands
Plants	Diet consisted mainly of meat and fish.	nuts, acorns, roots	beans, corn, cactus fruit, squash	corn, squash, beans	corn, squash, beans	berries, corn, squash, beans
Animals	elk, deer, bear, seal, whale, salmon	rabbit, pronghorn, salmon	rabbit, pronghorn	Diet was mainly vegetarian.	elk, deer	turkey, deer

C Indians got their food by hunting, gathering, fishing, or farming. Find the regions named above on the map below.

D Each Native American culture included many Indian nations. Differences in resources and climate led each group to rely on different types of food and shelter.

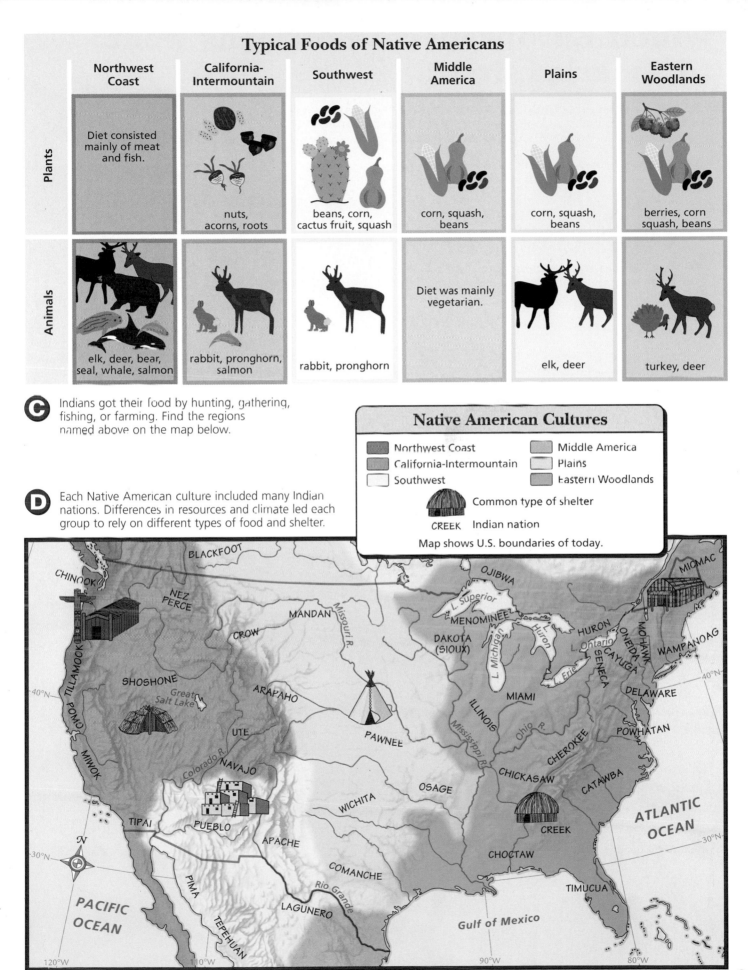

Native American Cultures

- Northwest Coast
- California-Intermountain
- Southwest
- Middle America
- Plains
- Eastern Woodlands

Common type of shelter

CREEK Indian nation

Map shows U.S. boundaries of today.

Which Europeans and Africans went to America first?

After 1492 the worlds of Europe, Africa, and America came together. The first white people in America came from Western Europe. The first black people there were slaves from West Africa.

▶ In both Europe and West Africa, monarchs ruled empires, kingdoms, and city-states. Warfare was common.

▶ European cities located near coasts became centers of trade, sea travel, and distant exploration.

▶ West African trade centers were inland. Many groups fought for control of valuable resources.

B Trade and valuable goods from overseas brought wealth to parts of European port cities such as Amsterdam, shown here.

A

Western Europe had easy access to the Atlantic Ocean. Voyages sponsored by Western European countries led to land claims and settlement in America and elsewhere.

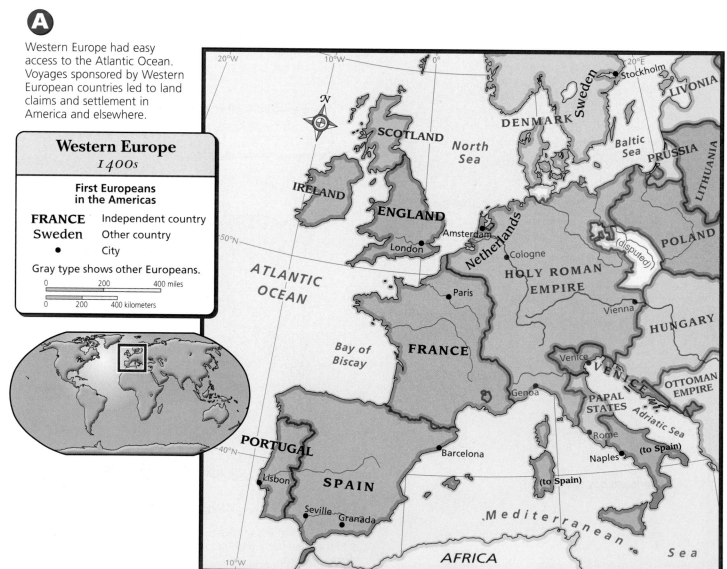

Western Europe
1400s

First Europeans in the Americas

FRANCE	Independent country
Sweden	Other country
•	City

Gray type shows other Europeans.

0   200   400 miles

0   200   400 kilometers

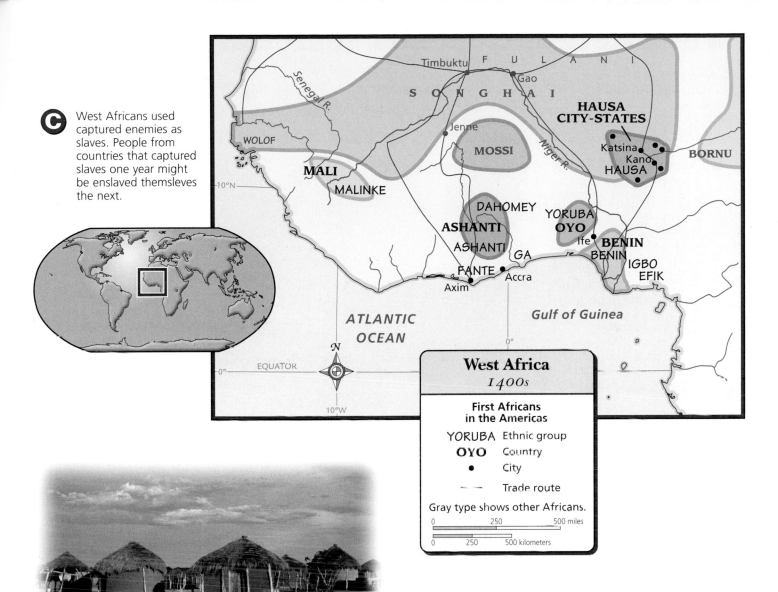

C West Africans used captured enemies as slaves. People from countries that captured slaves one year might be enslaved themsleves the next.

West Africa
1400s

First Africans in the Americas

YORUBA Ethnic group

OYO Country

• City

— Trade route

Gray type shows other Africans.

```
0        250        500 miles
0     250    500 kilometers
```

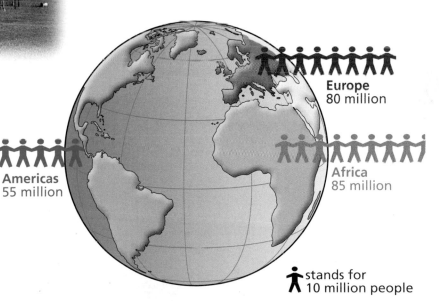

D Most West Africans lived in farming villages. Villagers worked together to raise animals and crops, and to defend themselves against enemy attacks and slave raids.

1444 Portuguese traders begin sailing to West Africa to buy slaves.

Americas 55 million

Europe 80 million

Africa 85 million

👤 stands for 10 million people

E **People in Three Worlds**

Until 1492 neither Europeans nor Africans were aware that the Americas—and the 55 million people who lived there—existed.

What were Europeans searching for?

For centuries Europeans traded for highly prized luxury goods from Southern and Eastern Asia. They referred to these distant regions of Asia as *the Indies*.

▶ The main trade route to the Indies was the Silk Road, which crossed all of Central Asia.

▶ Then in the late 1400s, Europe was blocked from using the Silk Road.

▶ The nations of Europe immediately began searching for a way of reaching the Indies by sea.

▶ Long voyages were made possible by new navigational skills and new shipbuilding technology.

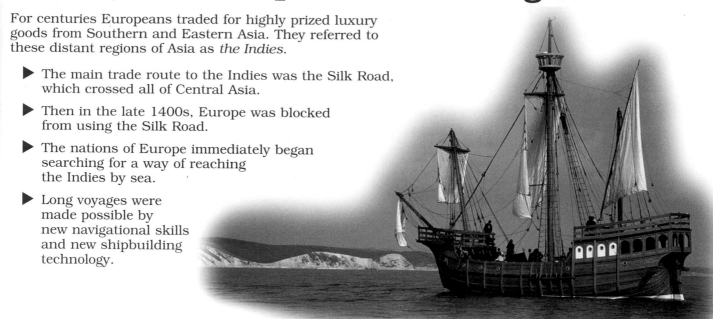

A Wealthy traders paid shipbuilders in Spain and Portugal for a new kind of ship called the *caravel*. Caravels held large amounts of cargo and were fast and easy to handle.

B Many of the goods from the Indies could be found nowhere else. For example, black pepper came from the Spice Islands. Where were the Spice Islands?

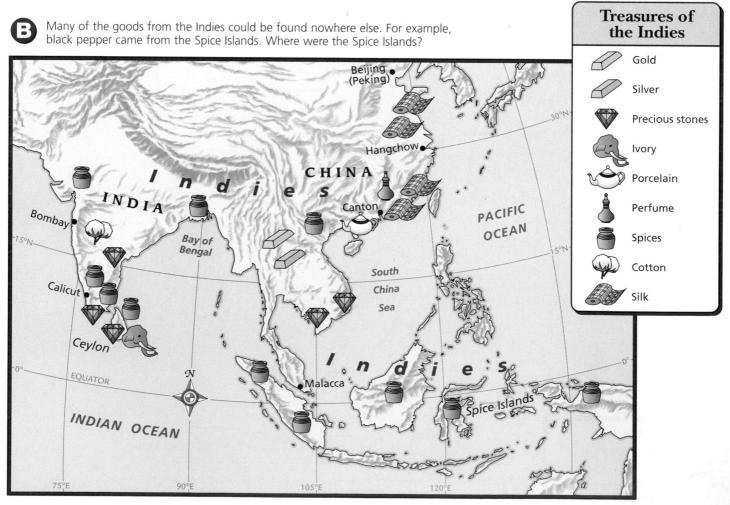

Treasures of the Indies

Gold

Silver

Precious stones

Ivory

Porcelain

Perfume

Spices

Cotton

Silk

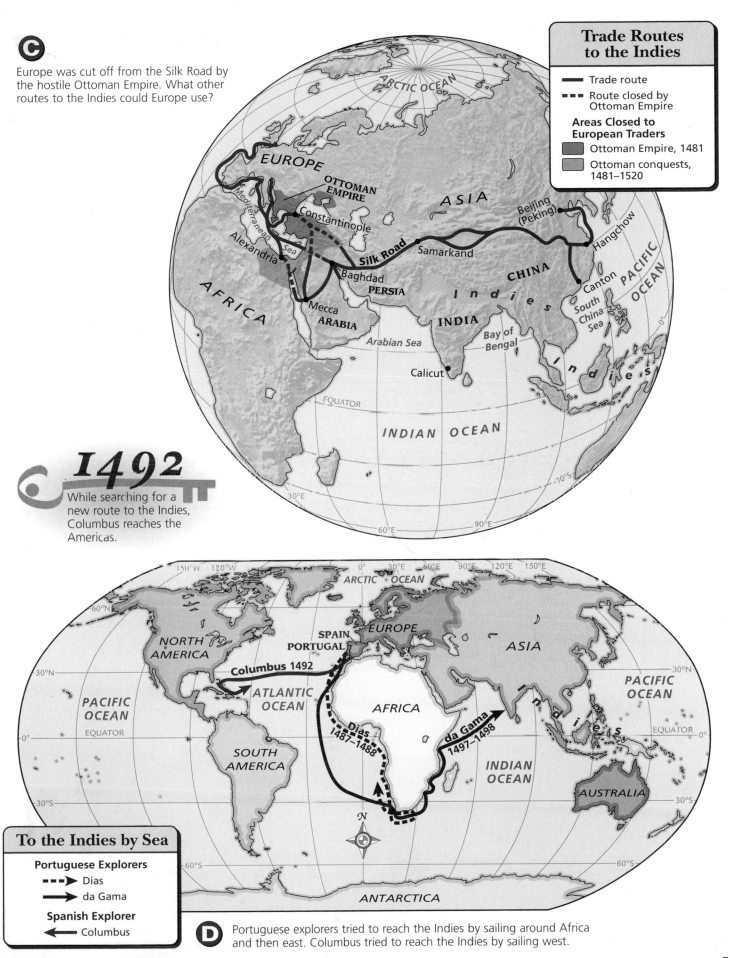

C Europe was cut off from the Silk Road by the hostile Ottoman Empire. What other routes to the Indies could Europe use?

Trade Routes to the Indies

— Trade route
- - - Route closed by Ottoman Empire

Areas Closed to European Traders
▨ Ottoman Empire, 1481
▨ Ottoman conquests, 1481–1520

ARCTIC OCEAN

EUROPE

OTTOMAN EMPIRE

Constantinople

Mediterranean Sea

Alexandria

AFRICA

Baghdad

Mecca

ARABIA

PERSIA

ASIA

Silk Road

Samarkand

Beijing (Peking)

Hangchow

CHINA

Canton

South China Sea

PACIFIC OCEAN

INDIA

Arabian Sea

Bay of Bengal

Calicut

I n d i e s

EQUATOR

INDIAN OCEAN

30°E 60°E 90°E

1492

While searching for a new route to the Indies, Columbus reaches the Americas.

150°W 120°W 0° 30°E 60°E 90°E 120°E 150°E

ARCTIC OCEAN

60°N

NORTH AMERICA

SPAIN
PORTUGAL

EUROPE

ASIA

30°N

Columbus 1492

ATLANTIC OCEAN

PACIFIC OCEAN

PACIFIC OCEAN

EQUATOR

SOUTH AMERICA

AFRICA

Dias 1487–1488

da Gama 1497–1498

INDIAN OCEAN

I n d i e s

AUSTRALIA

30°S

N

60°S

ANTARCTICA

To the Indies by Sea

Portuguese Explorers
- - - ▶ Dias
—— ▶ da Gama

Spanish Explorer
◀—— Columbus

D Portuguese explorers tried to reach the Indies by sailing around Africa and then east. Columbus tried to reach the Indies by sailing west.

Why did Europeans explore America?

Shortly after Columbus returned, other Europeans realized he had not reached the Indies. They began to think of the Americas as a "New World."

▶ Europeans claimed the parts of the New World they explored for the countries that sent them.

▶ Explorers kept trying to reach the Indies by going through or around North America.

▶ The Spanish soon stopped looking for the Indies and started searching for gold.

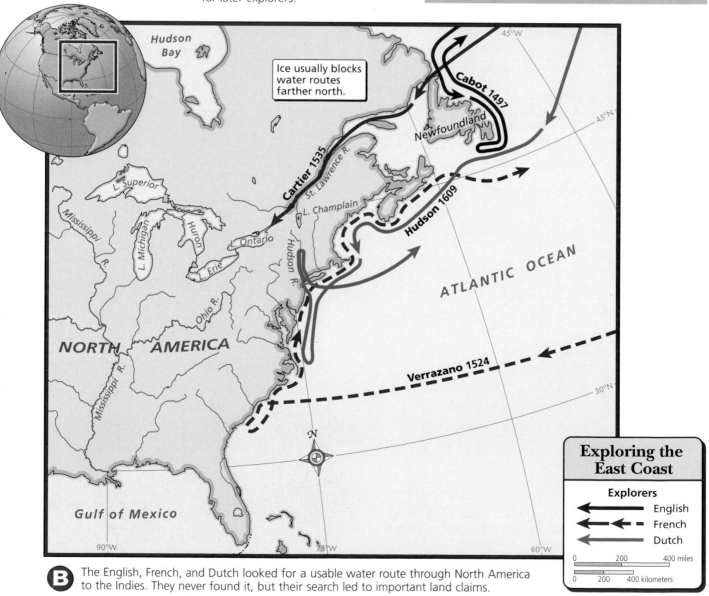

A Jacques Cartier and other early explorers lacked accurate maps. Information from their trips was used to make better maps for later explorers.

Ice usually blocks water routes farther north.

Hudson Bay

Cabot 1497

Newfoundland

Cartier 1535

St. Lawrence R.

L. Champlain

L. Superior

Mississippi R.

L. Michigan

Huron

L. Erie

L. Ontario

Hudson R.

Hudson 1609

Ohio R.

NORTH AMERICA

ATLANTIC OCEAN

Verrazano 1524

Gulf of Mexico

90°W

75°W

60°W

45°W

45°N

30°N

Exploring the East Coast

Explorers

→ English

⇢ French

→ Dutch

| 0 | 200 | 400 miles |
| 0 | 200 | 400 kilometers |

B The English, French, and Dutch looked for a usable water route through North America to the Indies. They never found it, but their search led to important land claims.

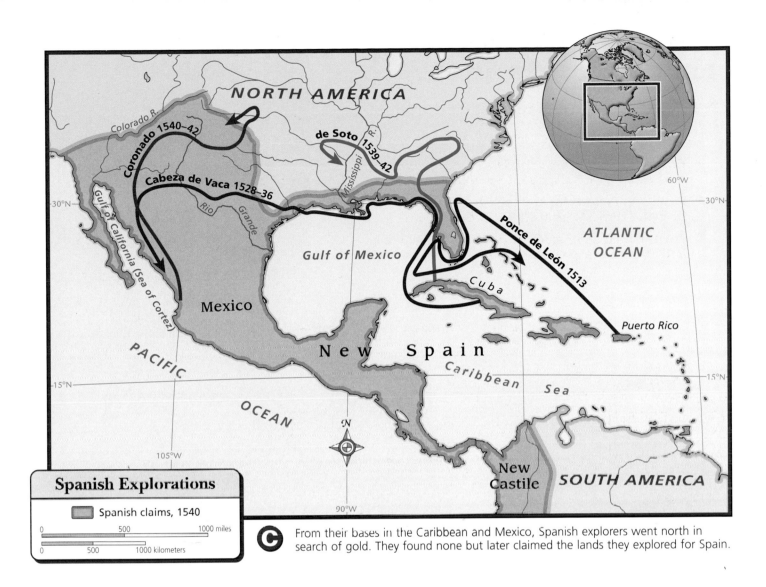

NORTH AMERICA

Colorado R.

Coronado 1540–42

de Soto 1539–42

Cabeza de Vaca 1528–36

Mississippi R.

Gulf of California (Sea of Cortez)

Rio Grande

30°N

Mexico

Gulf of Mexico

New Spain

Ponce de León 1513

ATLANTIC OCEAN

30°N

60°W

Cuba

Puerto Rico

PACIFIC

OCEAN

Caribbean Sea

15°N

15°N

105°W

New Castile

SOUTH AMERICA

90°W

Spanish Explorations

Spanish claims, 1540

0   500   1000 miles

0   500   1000 kilometers

C From their bases in the Caribbean and Mexico, Spanish explorers went north in search of gold. They found none but later claimed the lands they explored for Spain.

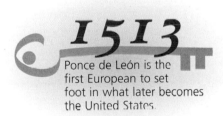

1513

Ponce de León is the first European to set foot in what later becomes the United States.

D

Juan Ponce de León was accompanied by priests as well as soldiers. The Spanish meant to conquer the Native Americans, but they also meant to convert them to Christianity.

15

What happened when three worlds met?

European and African contact with the Americas changed millions of lives around the world.

▶ Very soon after Europeans began settling the Americas, they began bringing Africans to work here as slaves.

▶ Plants and animals crossed the Atlantic Ocean in both directions on European ships.

▶ Millions of Native Americans died of unfamiliar diseases from the Eastern Hemisphere, such as smallpox and measles.

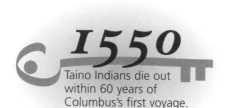

1550

Taino Indians die out within 60 years of Columbus's first voyage.

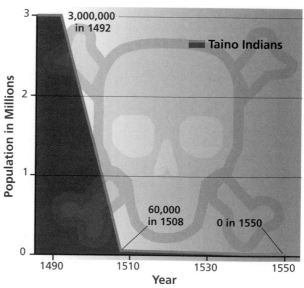

A **Death of the Taino**

After they were enslaved by the Spanish, the Taino Indians of the Caribbean died from smallpox or overwork. The Spanish replaced them with slaves from Africa.

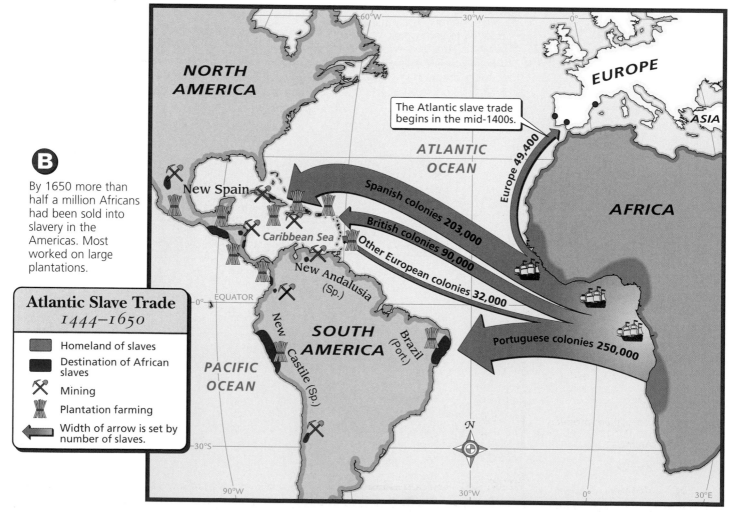

B

By 1650 more than half a million Africans had been sold into slavery in the Americas. Most worked on large plantations.

Atlantic Slave Trade
1444–1650

	Homeland of slaves
	Destination of African slaves
✗	Mining
🌾	Plantation farming
⬅	Width of arrow is set by number of slaves.

The Atlantic slave trade begins in the mid-1400s.

Europe 49,400

Spanish colonies 203,000

British colonies 90,000

Other European colonies 32,000

Portuguese colonies 250,000

New Spain

Caribbean Sea

New Andalusia (Sp.)

New Castile (Sp.)

Brazil (Port.)

NORTH AMERICA

SOUTH AMERICA

EUROPE

ASIA

AFRICA

ATLANTIC OCEAN

PACIFIC OCEAN

C

Before European contact with the Americas, only Native Americans raised corn. Today corn is widely grown around the world.

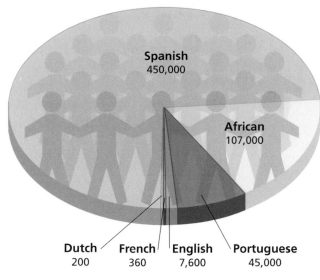

Spanish
450,000

African
107,000

Dutch
200

French
360

English
7,600

Portuguese
45,000

D **Newcomers to the Americas, 1625**

The Spanish began settling the Americas in 1496. By the 1600s there were eight times as many Spaniards in the Americas as all other European settlers combined.

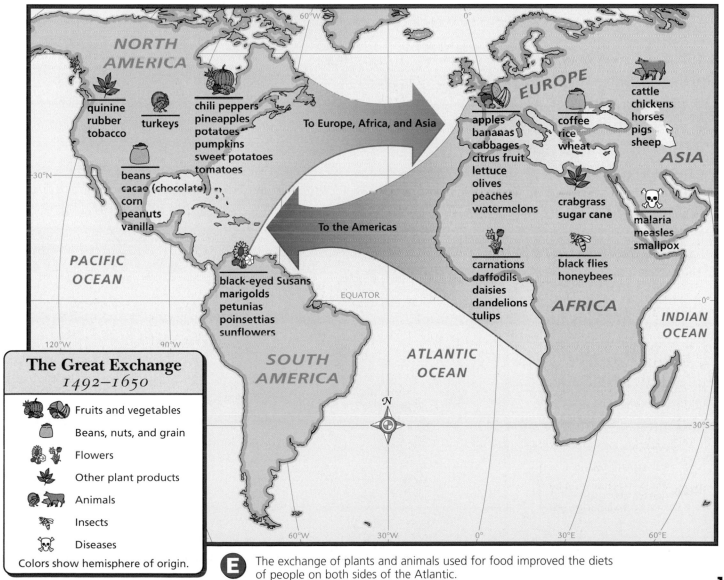

The Great Exchange
1492–1650

- Fruits and vegetables
- Beans, nuts, and grain
- Flowers
- Other plant products
- Animals
- Insects
- Diseases

Colors show hemisphere of origin.

NORTH AMERICA

quinine
rubber
tobacco

turkeys

chili peppers
pineapples
potatoes
pumpkins
sweet potatoes
tomatoes

To Europe, Africa, and Asia

beans
cacao (chocolate)
corn
peanuts
vanilla

PACIFIC OCEAN

black-eyed Susans
marigolds
petunias
poinsettias
sunflowers

To the Americas

EQUATOR

SOUTH AMERICA

ATLANTIC OCEAN

EUROPE

apples
bananas
cabbages
citrus fruit
lettuce
olives
peaches
watermelons

coffee
rice
wheat

cattle
chickens
horses
pigs
sheep

ASIA

crabgrass
sugar cane

malaria
measles
smallpox

carnations
daffodils
daisies
dandelions
tulips

black flies
honeybees

AFRICA

INDIAN OCEAN

E The exchange of plants and animals used for food improved the diets of people on both sides of the Atlantic.

Where did the Spanish settle?

Spain, England, and France all claimed land in North America. But Spain was the first to build settlements here.

▶ Explorers claimed what later became the Southeastern and Southwestern United States for Spain. Spain quickly built settlements in both regions.

▶ Some Spanish settlements began as *presidios*, or forts. They protected Spanish settlers and travelers.

▶ Other Spanish settlements began as *missions*, where priests converted Indians to the Roman Catholic religion.

▶ The Spanish word for "town" is *pueblo*. The Spanish used it for both Spanish and Indian settlements.

1565

Spain establishes St. Augustine, Florida, the oldest permanent European settlement in the United States.

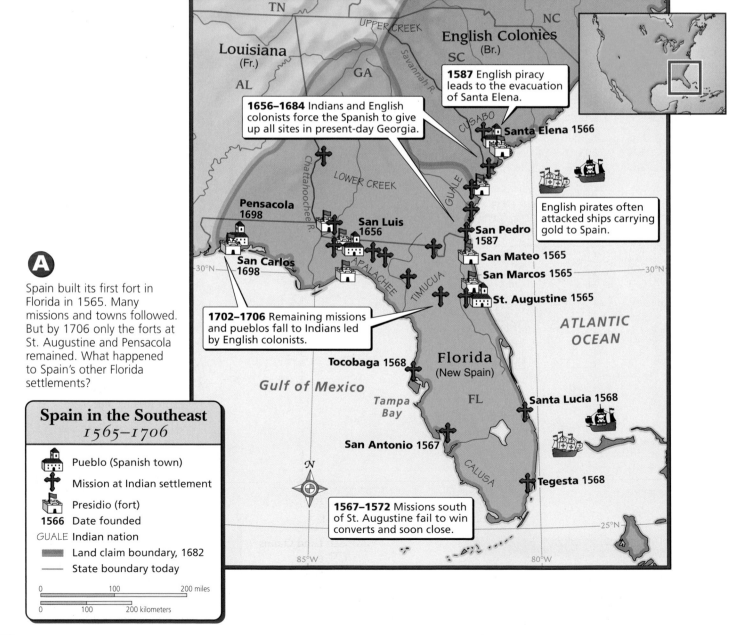

A

Spain built its first fort in Florida in 1565. Many missions and towns followed. But by 1706 only the forts at St. Augustine and Pensacola remained. What happened to Spain's other Florida settlements?

1656–1684 Indians and English colonists force the Spanish to give up all sites in present-day Georgia.

1587 English piracy leads to the evacuation of Santa Elena.

Santa Elena 1566

English pirates often attacked ships carrying gold to Spain.

Pensacola 1698

San Luis 1656

San Pedro 1587

San Mateo 1565

San Marcos 1565

San Carlos 1698

St. Augustine 1565

1702–1706 Remaining missions and pueblos fall to Indians led by English colonists.

ATLANTIC OCEAN

Tocobaga 1568

Florida (New Spain)

Gulf of Mexico

Tampa Bay

FL

Santa Lucia 1568

San Antonio 1567

Tegesta 1568

1567–1572 Missions south of St. Augustine fail to win converts and soon close.

Spain in the Southeast
1565–1706

🏛	Pueblo (Spanish town)
✝	Mission at Indian settlement
🏰	Presidio (fort)
1566	Date founded
GUALE	Indian nation
▬	Land claim boundary, 1682
—	State boundary today

0   100   200 miles
0   100   200 kilometers

TN
Louisiana (Fr.)
AL
GA
UPPER CREEK
Savannah R.
NC
English Colonies (Br.)
SC
CUSABO
Chattahoochee R.
LOWER CREEK
GUALE
APALACHEE
TIMUCUA
30°N
CALUSA

85°W   80°W   25°N

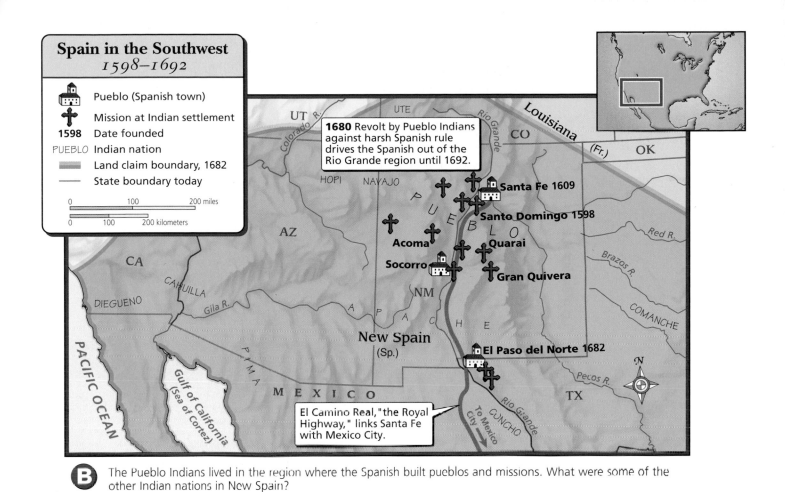

Spain in the Southwest
1598–1692

🏛️ Pueblo (Spanish town)

✝️ Mission at Indian settlement

1598 Date founded

PUEBLO Indian nation

▬ Land claim boundary, 1682

— State boundary today

0   100   200 miles
0 100 200 kilometers

1680 Revolt by Pueblo Indians against harsh Spanish rule drives the Spanish out of the Rio Grande region until 1692.

UT R.   UTE   Rio Grande   Louisiana
CO   (Fr.)   OK
HOPI   NAVAJO   P U E B L O   Santa Fe 1609
Colorado   Santo Domingo 1598   Red R.
AZ   Acoma   Quarai   Brazos R.
CA   Socorro   Gran Quivera   COMANCHE
CAHUILLA   A P A C H E
DIEGUENO   Gila R.   NM
New Spain   El Paso del Norte 1682
(Sp.)   Pecos R.
PACIFIC OCEAN   P I M A   M E X I C O   TX
Gulf of California (Sea of Cortez)   Rio Grande   CONCHO   To Mexico City

El Camino Real, "the Royal Highway," links Santa Fe with Mexico City.

B The Pueblo Indians lived in the region where the Spanish built pueblos and missions. What were some of the other Indian nations in New Spain?

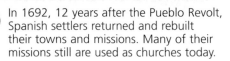

C In 1692, 12 years after the Pueblo Revolt, Spanish settlers returned and rebuilt their towns and missions. Many of their missions still are used as churches today.

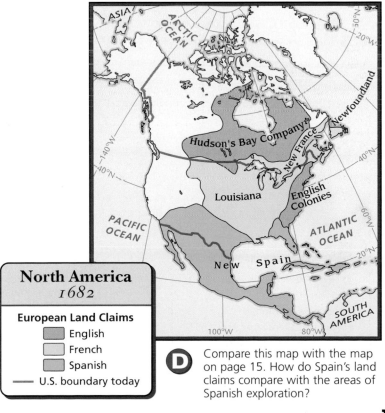

North America
1682

European Land Claims

▬ English
▬ French
▬ Spanish
— U.S. boundary today

ASIA   ARCTIC OCEAN   30°W   20°W
Hudson's Bay Company   New France   Newfoundland
Louisiana   English Colonies   40°N
PACIFIC OCEAN   ATLANTIC OCEAN   60°W
New Spain   20°N
100°W   80°W   SOUTH AMERICA

D Compare this map with the map on page 15. How do Spain's land claims compare with the areas of Spanish exploration?

Where did the English and other Europeans settle?

Like Spain, other European countries were eager to colonize the Americas. Early settlers hoped to find gold and silver, but they often made their fortunes in fur and tobacco.

▶ The English settled along much of the Atlantic coast. They usually lived in farming communities.

▶ The French settled in the North. Unlike the English, they preferred fur trading to farming.

▶ Dutch farmers and Swedish fur traders settled along the middle Atlantic coast.

1585

Roanoke Island becomes the first English colony in the Americas. Roanoke settlers vanish by 1590.

A

The English who settled in and near Massachusetts were looking for the freedom to practice their own religion. Other English, French, Dutch, and Swedish settlers came for trade and profit.

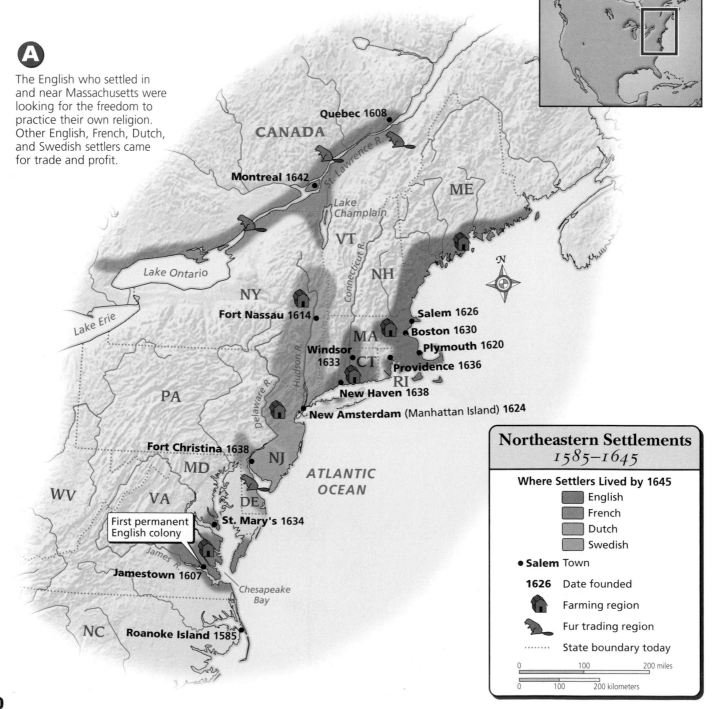

Quebec 1608

CANADA

Montreal 1642

St. Lawrence R.

Lake Champlain

ME

VT

Lake Ontario

NH

Connecticut R.

Lake Erie

NY

Fort Nassau 1614

Salem 1626

Boston 1630

MA

Plymouth 1620

Windsor 1633

CT

Providence 1636

Hudson R.

New Haven 1638

RI

New Amsterdam (Manhattan Island) **1624**

PA

Delaware R.

Fort Christina 1638

NJ

MD

ATLANTIC OCEAN

WV

VA

DE

First permanent English colony

St. Mary's 1634

James R.

Jamestown 1607

Chesapeake Bay

NC

Roanoke Island 1585

Northeastern Settlements
1585–1645

Where Settlers Lived by 1645

- English
- French
- Dutch
- Swedish

● **Salem** Town

1626 Date founded

🏠 Farming region

🦫 Fur trading region

⋯⋯⋯ State boundary today

0   100   200 miles
0   100   200 kilometers

See the map on page 20 for Jamestown's location.

B

In 1607 English settlers built Jamestown on a peninsula in Virginia. The colony made a profit after the settlers cleared fields and grew tobacco.

Jamestown
1607

1. Church
2. Market area
3. Storehouse
4. Courthouse
5. Cannon

Other buildings are houses.

James River

to the Atlantic Ocean

N

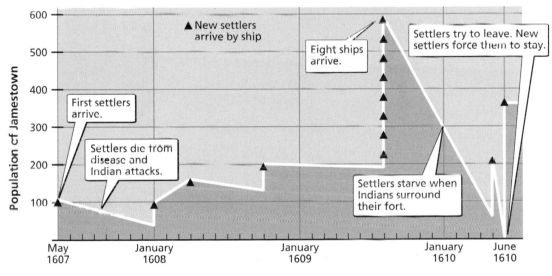

Population of Jamestown

▲ New settlers arrive by ship

First settlers arrive.

Settlers die from disease and Indian attacks.

Fight ships arrive.

Settlers try to leave. New settlers force them to stay.

Settlers starve when Indians surround their fort.

May 1607 | January 1608 | January 1609 | January 1610 | June 1610

C

Population of Jamestown

Jamestown eventually thrived. But most of its first settlers, like other early colonists, died from disease, starvation, or conflicts with Indians. Describe its losses between 1607 and 1610.

D

The Dutch purchased Manhattan Island from the Indians for $24 in goods. The small Dutch farming community on the island was called New Amsterdam. Later it became New York City.

Which colonies became the United States?

The United States began as 13 colonies along the Atlantic coast of North America.

▶ The English founded most of the colonies in the 1600s. But there were colonists from other countries too.

▶ In 1707 England became part of Great Britain. From then on the colonies were referred to as *British*.

▶ Many of the early colonists left Europe in search of religious freedom.

▶ Africans were brought to the colonies against their will and sold into slavery.

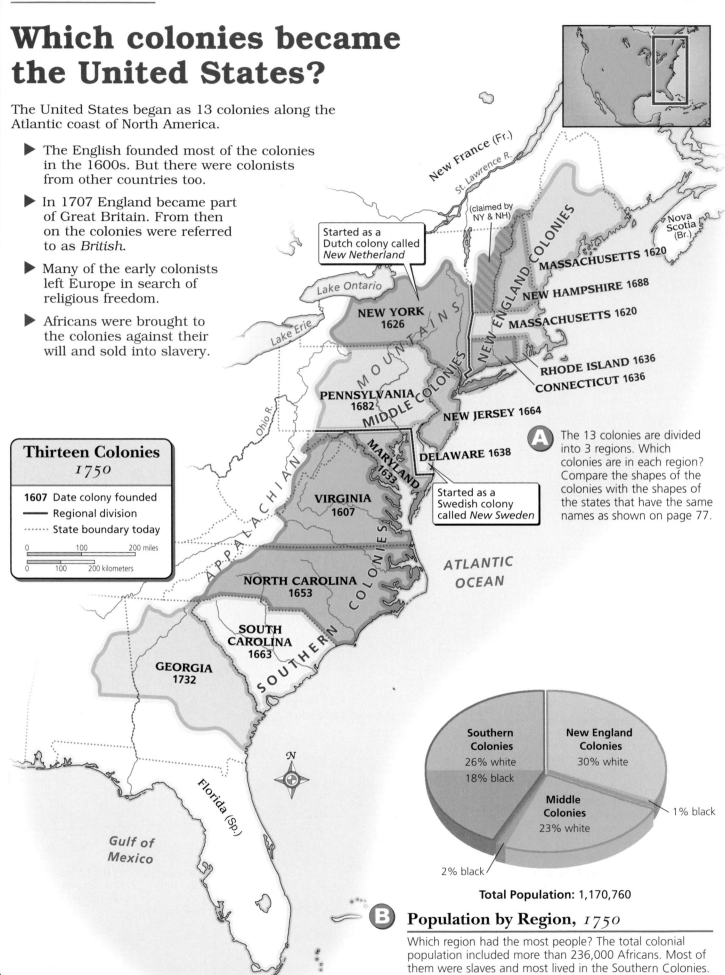

Started as a Dutch colony called *New Netherland*

Started as a Swedish colony called *New Sweden*

MASSACHUSETTS 1620
NEW HAMPSHIRE 1688
MASSACHUSETTS 1620
RHODE ISLAND 1636
CONNECTICUT 1636

NEW YORK 1626
PENNSYLVANIA 1682
NEW JERSEY 1664
DELAWARE 1638
MARYLAND 1633
VIRGINIA 1607
NORTH CAROLINA 1653
SOUTH CAROLINA 1663
GEORGIA 1732

New France (Fr.)
St. Lawrence R.
(claimed by NY & NH)
Nova Scotia (Br.)
Lake Ontario
Lake Erie
Ohio R.
MOUNTAINS
APPALACHIAN
MIDDLE COLONIES
NEW ENGLAND COLONIES
SOUTHERN COLONIES
ATLANTIC OCEAN
Florida (Sp.)
Gulf of Mexico

Thirteen Colonies
1750

1607 Date colony founded
— Regional division
···· State boundary today

0   100   200 miles
0   100   200 kilometers

A The 13 colonies are divided into 3 regions. Which colonies are in each region? Compare the shapes of the colonies with the shapes of the states that have the same names as shown on page 77.

Southern Colonies
26% white
18% black

New England Colonies
30% white

Middle Colonies
23% white

1% black

2% black

Total Population: 1,170,760

B **Population by Region,** *1750*

Which region had the most people? The total colonial population included more than 236,000 Africans. Most of them were slaves and most lived in the Southern Colonies.

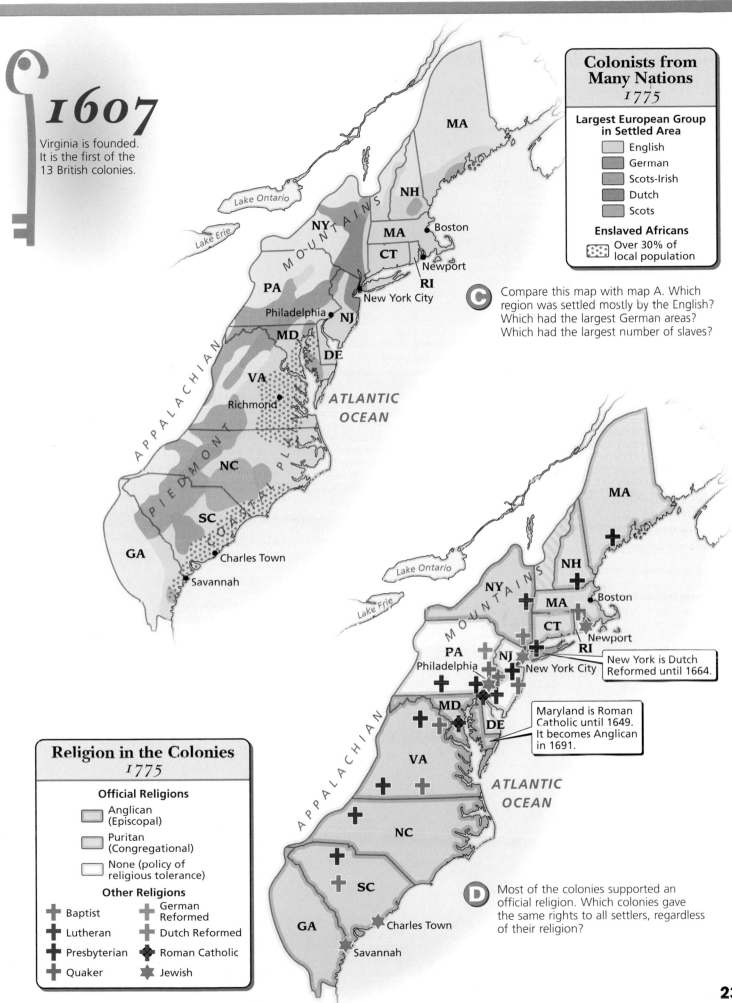

1607

Virginia is founded. It is the first of the 13 British colonies.

Colonists from Many Nations
1775

Largest European Group in Settled Area

- English
- German
- Scots-Irish
- Dutch
- Scots

Enslaved Africans

- Over 30% of local population

C Compare this map with map A. Which region was settled mostly by the English? Which had the largest German areas? Which had the largest number of slaves?

Lake Ontario

Lake Erie

MOUNTAINS

MA

NH

MA • Boston

CT

NY

RI

PA

New York City

Philadelphia NJ

MD

DE

VA

Richmond

ATLANTIC OCEAN

APPALACHIAN

PIEDMONT

NC

COASTAL PL.

SC

GA • Charles Town

• Savannah

Religion in the Colonies
1775

Official Religions

- Anglican (Episcopal)
- Puritan (Congregational)
- None (policy of religious tolerance)

Other Religions

✚ Baptist	✚ German Reformed
✚ Lutheran	✚ Dutch Reformed
✚ Presbyterian	◆ Roman Catholic
✚ Quaker	★ Jewish

MA

NY

MOUNTAINS

NH

MA • Boston

CT

Lake Ontario

Lake Erie

RI • Newport

PA

NJ

New York City

Philadelphia

New York is Dutch Reformed until 1664.

MD

DE

Maryland is Roman Catholic until 1649. It becomes Anglican in 1691.

VA

ATLANTIC OCEAN

APPALACHIAN

NC

SC

GA • Charles Town

• Savannah

D Most of the colonies supported an official religion. Which colonies gave the same rights to all settlers, regardless of their religion?

23

Which were the New England Colonies?

The New England Colonies were Connecticut, Rhode Island, Massachusetts, and New Hampshire.

▶ New England settlers were mainly English Puritans. They came seeking the freedom to practice their own religion.

▶ Most New Englanders made a living by farming, fishing, hunting whales, or building ships.

▶ Many villages required settlers to attend religious services and pay taxes to support the churches.

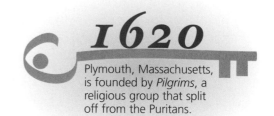

1620

Plymouth, Massachusetts, is founded by *Pilgrims*, a religious group that split off from the Puritans.

Ⓐ Which was the first New England settlement? Which rivers had towns far from the Atlantic coast? Use this map with map B to find settled areas that did not have large towns.

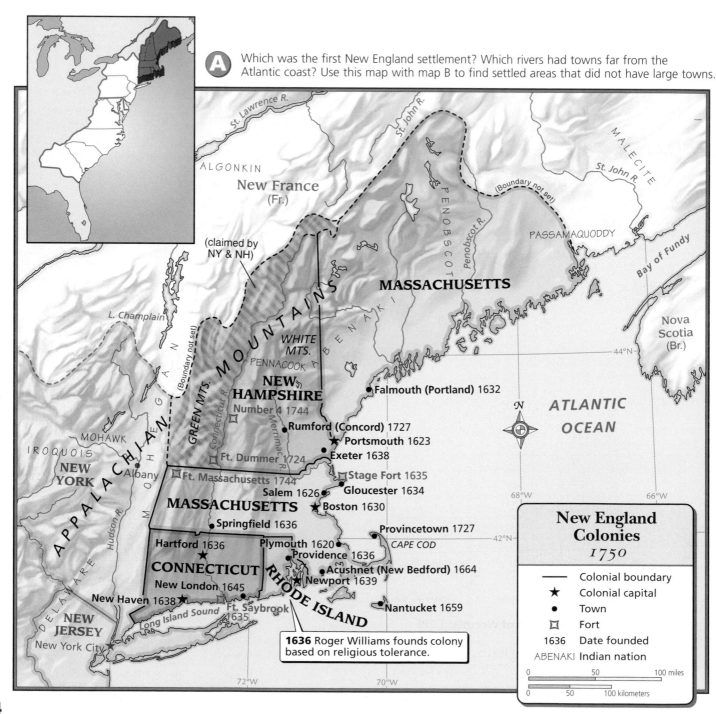

1636 Roger Williams founds colony based on religious tolerance.

New England Colonies
1750

——	Colonial boundary
★	Colonial capital
●	Town
⬚	Fort
1636	Date founded
ABENAKI	Indian nation

0   50   100 miles
0   50   100 kilometers

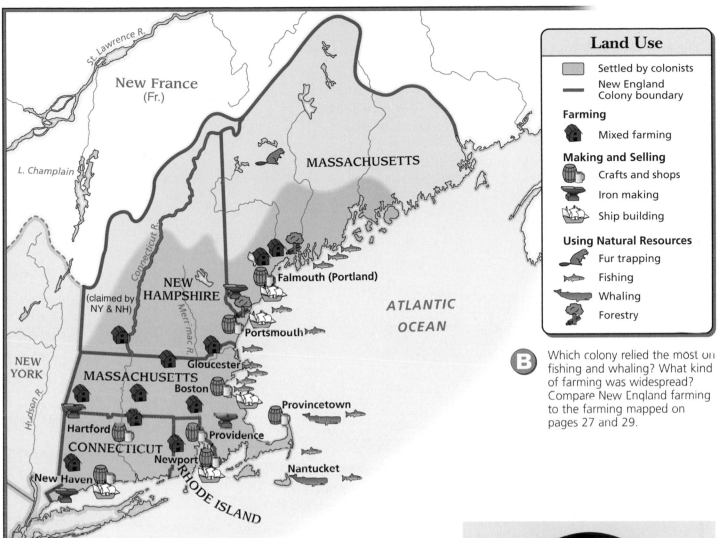

New France
(Fr.)

L. Champlain

MASSACHUSETTS

St. Lawrence R.

Connecticut R.

NEW
HAMPSHIRE
(claimed by
NY & NH)

Merrimac R.

Falmouth (Portland)

ATLANTIC
OCEAN

Portsmouth

NEW
YORK

Hudson R.

Gloucester

MASSACHUSETTS
Boston

Provincetown

Hartford

CONNECTICUT

Providence

New Haven

Newport

RHODE ISLAND

Nantucket

NEW
JERSEY

Land Use

	Settled by colonists
	New England Colony boundary

Farming

Mixed farming

Making and Selling

Crafts and shops

Iron making

Ship building

Using Natural Resources

Fur trapping

Fishing

Whaling

Forestry

B Which colony relied the most on fishing and whaling? What kind of farming was widespread? Compare New England farming to the farming mapped on pages 27 and 29.

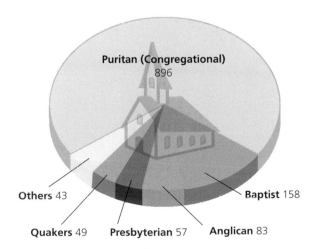

Puritan (Congregational)
896

Others 43

Baptist 158

Quakers 49   Presbyterian 57   Anglican 83

Total Houses of Worship: 1,286

C ## Religion in New England, *1775*

Anglicans were members of the official Church of England. Puritans, Baptists, and Quakers were members of English movements that had split off from the official church.

D Colonial children helped their families with daily chores. This actor at a historical site shows how children gathered firewood.

Which were the Middle Colonies?

The Middle Colonies were New York, Pennsylvania, New Jersey, and Delaware.

▶ The first settlers in the Middle Colonies were from the Netherlands and Sweden. English settlers arrived later.

▶ Long after the English took over, the Dutch (from the Netherlands) outnumbered them in New York and New Jersey.

▶ No American colonies were founded by Germans, but German settlers were the largest group in much of Pennsylvania.

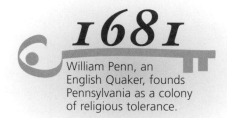

1681

William Penn, an English Quaker, founds Pennsylvania as a colony of religious tolerance.

A Which cities in New York and Delaware were founded by Dutch and Swedish settlers? Which of the capitals of these colonies are state capitals today?

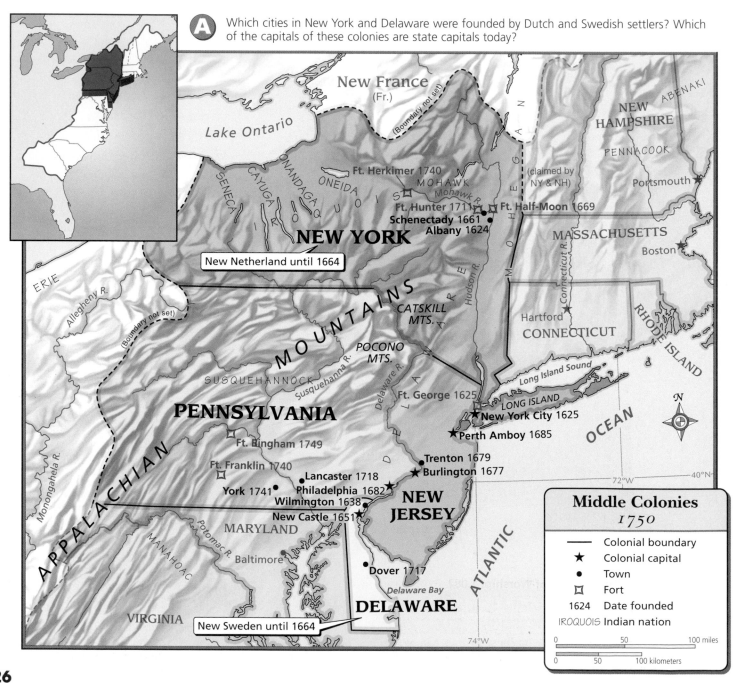

New France (Fr.)

(Boundary not set)

Lake Ontario

NEW HAMPSHIRE

ABENAKI

PENNACOOK

Portsmouth

SENECA CAYUGA ONONDAGA ONEIDA

IROQUOIS

MOHAWK

Ft. Herkimer 1740

Mohawk R.

(claimed by NY & NH)

Ft. Hunter 1711

Ft. Half-Moon 1669

Schenectady 1661

Albany 1624

MASSACHUSETTS

Boston

NEW YORK

New Netherland until 1664

ERIE

Allegheny R.

(Boundary not set)

CATSKILL MTS.

Hudson R.

MOHEGAN

Connecticut R.

Hartford

CONNECTICUT

RHODE ISLAND

M O U N T A I N S

POCONO MTS.

SUSQUEHANNOCK

Susquehanna R.

Delaware R.

Long Island Sound

LONG ISLAND

PENNSYLVANIA

Ft. Bingham 1749

Ft. George 1625

New York City 1625

Perth Amboy 1685

OCEAN

N

Ft. Franklin 1740

Trenton 1679

Burlington 1677

72°W

40°N

Lancaster 1718

York 1741 Philadelphia 1682

Wilmington 1638

New Castle 1651

NEW JERSEY

APPALACHIAN

Monongahela R.

MANAHOAC

MARYLAND

Potomac R. Baltimore

Dover 1717

Delaware Bay

ATLANTIC

VIRGINIA

New Sweden until 1664

DELAWARE

74°W

Middle Colonies 1750	
——	Colonial boundary
★	Colonial capital
•	Town
⌂	Fort
1624	Date founded
IROQUOIS	Indian nation

0   50   100 miles

0   50   100 kilometers

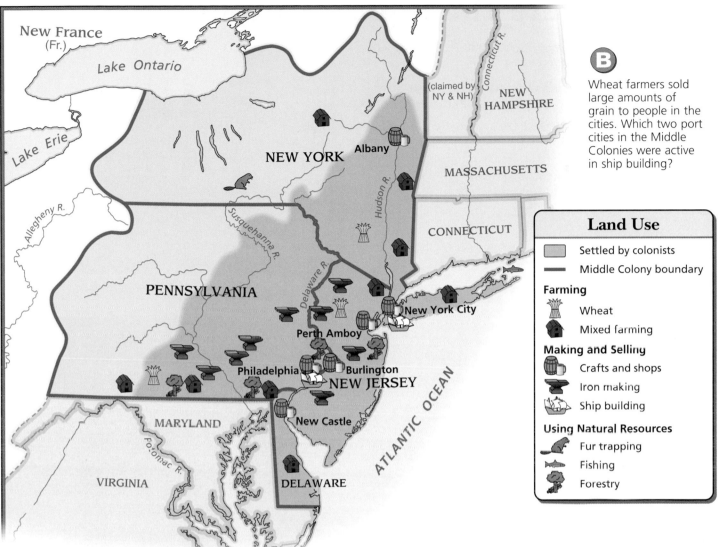

New France
(Fr.)

Lake Ontario

Lake Erie

Allegheny R.

NEW YORK

Albany

Hudson R.

Susquehanna R.

Delaware R.

PENNSYLVANIA

Perth Amboy

Philadelphia

Burlington

NEW JERSEY

New Castle

MARYLAND

Potomac R.

VIRGINIA

DELAWARE

(claimed by NY & NH)

NEW HAMPSHIRE

Connecticut R.

MASSACHUSETTS

CONNECTICUT

New York City

ATLANTIC OCEAN

Land Use

- Settled by colonists
- Middle Colony boundary

Farming
- Wheat
- Mixed farming

Making and Selling
- Crafts and shops
- Iron making
- Ship building

Using Natural Resources
- Fur trapping
- Fishing
- Forestry

B Wheat farmers sold large amounts of grain to people in the cities. Which two port cities in the Middle Colonies were active in ship building?

Religion in the Middle Colonies, 1775

Quaker 148
Anglican 127
Dutch Reformed 118
German Reformed 105
Presbyterian 274
Lutheran 102
Others 115
Baptist 93

Total Houses of Worship: 1,082

C **Religion in the Middle Colonies,** *1775*

The English made New York officially Anglican, but Dutch settlers belonged to other churches. The other three colonies were tolerant of all faiths. Compare this graph with the one on page 25.

D New York, shown here, and Philadelphia were the largest cities in the colonies. Port cities were important centers of trade and manufacturing.

Which were the Southern Colonies?

The Southern Colonies were Maryland, Virginia, North Carolina, South Carolina, and Georgia.

▶ The first Southern colonists were wealthy Englishmen who started large one-crop farms called *plantations*.

▶ Later settlers included Germans, Scots, and Scots-Irish who had smaller farms farther inland.

▶ Although the Southern Colonies were officially Anglican, most of the colonists practiced other faiths.

1732
Georgia is founded as the 13th and final British colony.

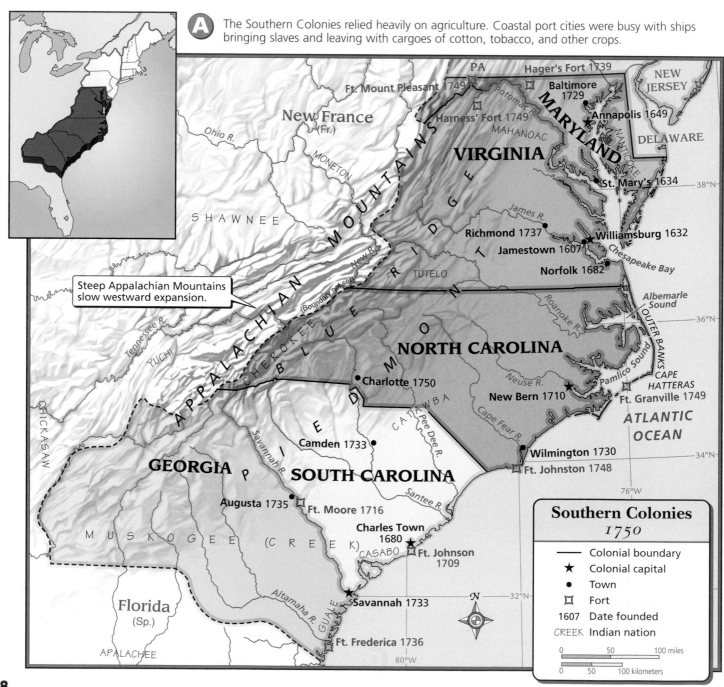

A The Southern Colonies relied heavily on agriculture. Coastal port cities were busy with ships bringing slaves and leaving with cargoes of cotton, tobacco, and other crops.

Steep Appalachian Mountains slow westward expansion.

Southern Colonies
1750

——	Colonial boundary
★	Colonial capital
●	Town
⛫	Fort
1607	Date founded
CREEK	Indian nation

0   50   100 miles
0   50   100 kilometers

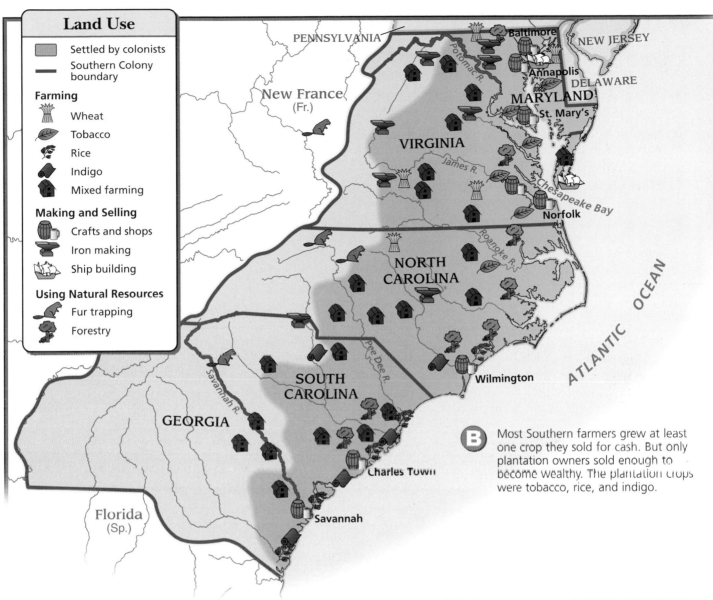

Land Use

- Settled by colonists
- Southern Colony boundary

Farming
- Wheat
- Tobacco
- Rice
- Indigo
- Mixed farming

Making and Selling
- Crafts and shops
- Iron making
- Ship building

Using Natural Resources
- Fur trapping
- Forestry

PENNSYLVANIA

NEW JERSEY

Baltimore

New France
(Fr.)

Annapolis

DELAWARE

Potomac R.

St. Mary's

MARYLAND

VIRGINIA

James R.

Chesapeake Bay

Norfolk

Roanoke R.

NORTH
CAROLINA

ATLANTIC OCEAN

SOUTH
CAROLINA

Pee Dee R.

GEORGIA

Savannah R.

Wilmington

Charles Town

Florida
(Sp.)

Savannah

B Most Southern farmers grew at least one crop they sold for cash. But only plantation owners sold enough to become wealthy. The plantation crops were tobacco, rice, and indigo.

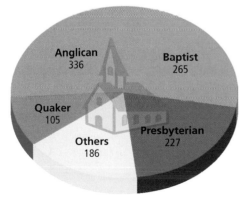

Religion in the Southern Colonies, *1775*

Anglican 336
Baptist 265
Quaker 105
Others 186
Presbyterian 227

Total Houses of Worship: 1,119

C Many Southern Anglicans lived near the coast. Other faiths were more common in inland cities and towns. Compare this graph with the graphs on pages 25 and 27.

D In the South, the wealthiest whites and most blacks lived and worked on plantations. Most white Southerners lived on smaller farms and did not own slaves.

Where did slaves work in the Thirteen Colonies?

Slaves were brought from Africa to America very early in the colonial period. By the 1700s, there were slaves throughout the British colonies.

► Slaves in America were originally taken from homelands in agricultural West Africa.

► More slaves were used in the Southern Colonies than in the others.

► Slave labor was used to produce some of the most valuable trade goods of the colonies.

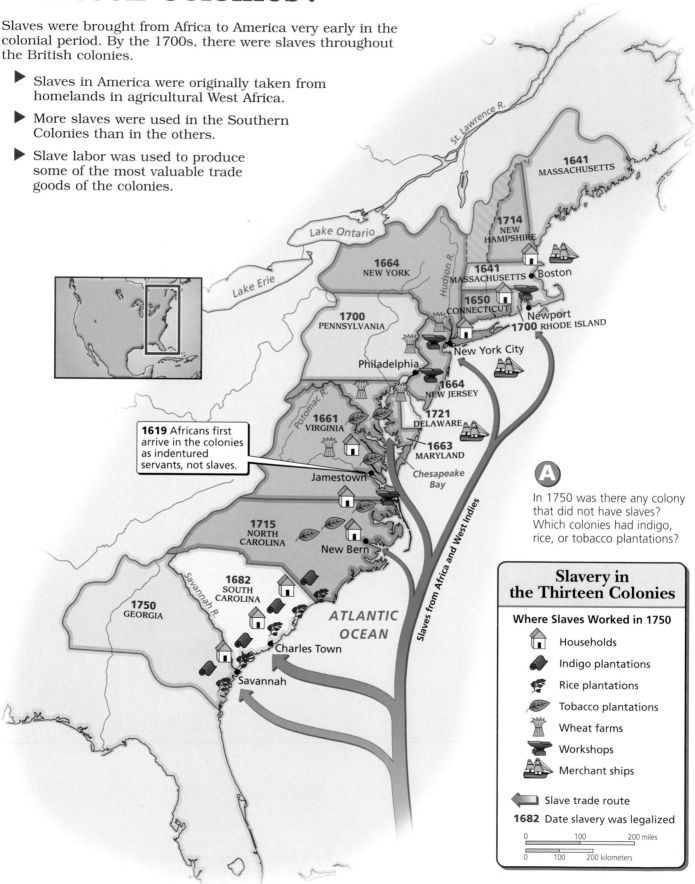

1619 Africans first arrive in the colonies as indentured servants, not slaves.

A

In 1750 was there any colony that did not have slaves? Which colonies had indigo, rice, or tobacco plantations?

Slavery in the Thirteen Colonies

Where Slaves Worked in 1750

🏠	Households
	Indigo plantations
	Rice plantations
	Tobacco plantations
	Wheat farms
	Workshops
	Merchant ships
←	Slave trade route
1682	Date slavery was legalized

0   100   200 miles

0   100   200 kilometers

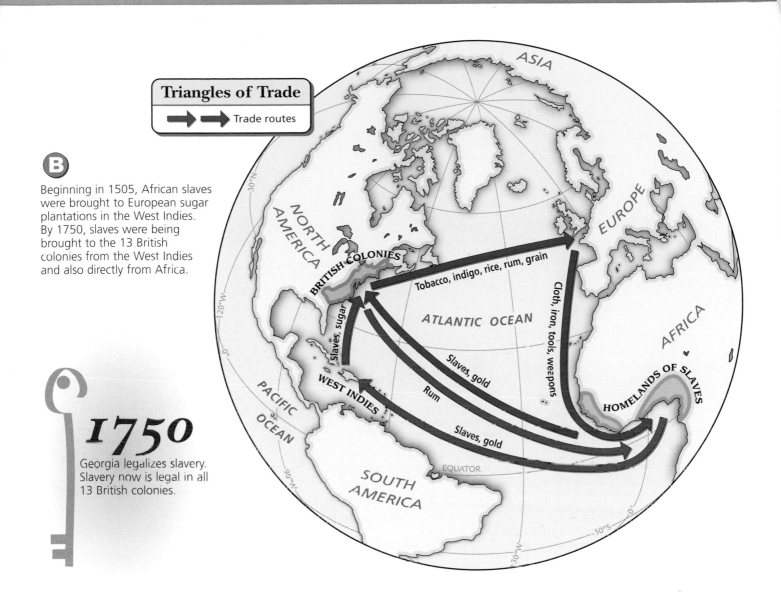

Triangles of Trade

→ → Trade routes

ASIA

B

Beginning in 1505, African slaves were brought to European sugar plantations in the West Indies. By 1750, slaves were being brought to the 13 British colonies from the West Indies and also directly from Africa.

EUROPE

NORTH AMERICA

BRITISH COLONIES

Tobacco, indigo, rice, rum, grain

ATLANTIC OCEAN

AFRICA

Cloth, iron, tools, weapons

Slaves, sugar

HOMELANDS OF SLAVES

WEST INDIES

Slaves, gold

Rum

Slaves, gold

PACIFIC OCEAN

EQUATOR

SOUTH AMERICA

1750

Georgia legalizes slavery. Slavery now is legal in all 13 British colonies.

Share of Exports in 1880

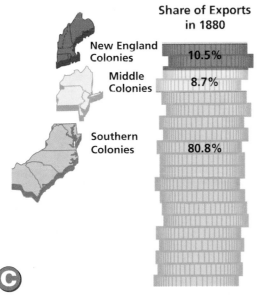

New England Colonies 10.5%

Middle Colonies 8.7%

Southern Colonies 80.8%

C

Colonial Exports to Great Britain, *1770*

The Southern Colonies could sell cash crops in such large amounts only by relying on unpaid slave labor.

D On both small farms and large plantations, slaves did the hard labor of plowing, planting, and harvesting by hand. In this photo, an actress portrays a slave at a historic site.

What led to the Revolutionary War?

Although the 13 colonies were British territory, each one made its own rules and laws.

▶ In 1763 Britain won the French and Indian War and forced France from North America.

▶ After the war, Britain tried to increase its control over the colonies. One way it did this was by taxing them for the first time.

▶ Colonists also were forbidden to settle beyond the Proclamation Line, a boundary drawn by the British.

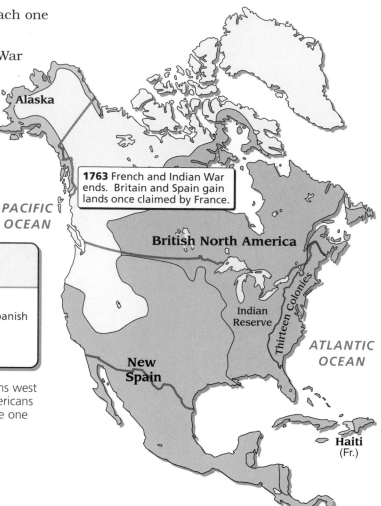

1763 French and Indian War ends. Britain and Spain gain lands once claimed by France.

PACIFIC OCEAN

Alaska

British North America

Indian Reserve

Thirteen Colonies

New Spain

ATLANTIC OCEAN

Haiti (Fr.)

North America
1763

European Land Claims

☐ British	☐ French	☐ Russian	☐ Spanish

——— Proclamation Line of 1763
——— U.S. boundary today

A In 1763 Britain reserved former French claims west of the Proclamation Line for the Native Americans who lived there. Compare this map with the one on page 19.

1764 MOLASSES — **Sugar Act** New tax on molasses

1765 — **Stamp Act** New taxes on newspapers, dice, playing cards, legal documents

1767 — **Townshend Act** New taxes on imported paint, lead, glass, paper, tea

1773 — **Tea Act** New tax on tea

B **British Taxes on the Colonists**

Great Britain paid its war debts by taxing goods that colonists depended on.

C In 1770 a protest against the presence of British troops in Boston turned violent. The soldiers opened fire and killed five colonists in what became known as the Boston Massacre.

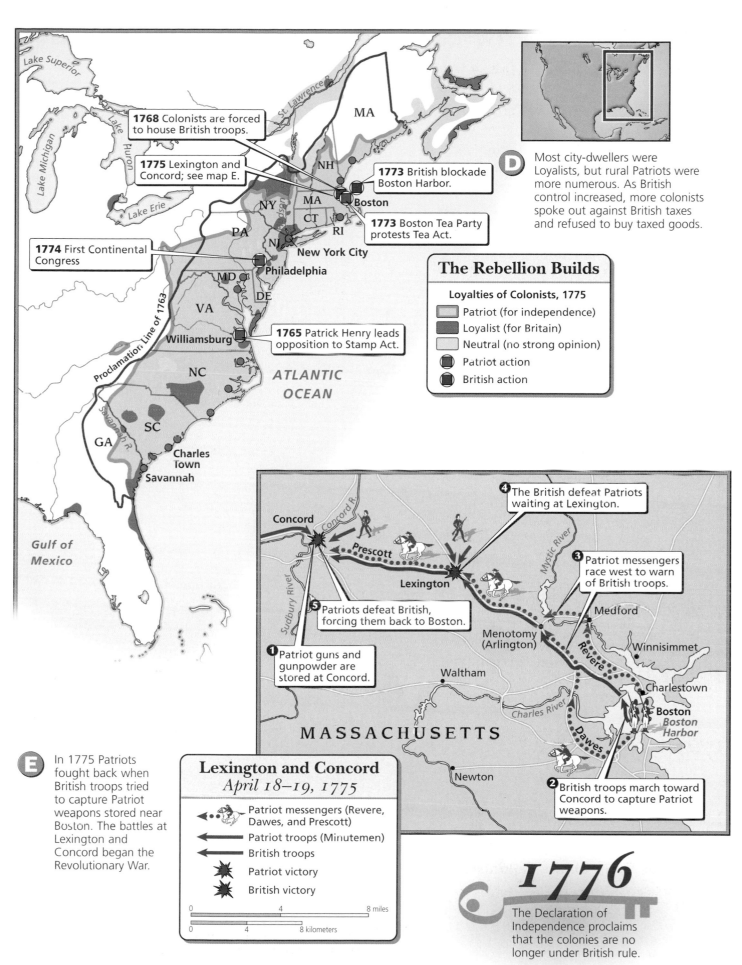

1768 Colonists are forced to house British troops.

1775 Lexington and Concord; see map E.

1773 British blockade Boston Harbor.

1774 First Continental Congress

1773 Boston Tea Party protests Tea Act.

1765 Patrick Henry leads opposition to Stamp Act.

Lake Superior

Lake Michigan

Lake Huron

Lake Erie

St. Lawrence

MA

NH

NY

MA

CT

RI

PA

NJ

New York City

Philadelphia

MD

DE

VA

Williamsburg

Proclamation Line of 1763

NC

ATLANTIC OCEAN

Savannah R.

SC

GA

Charles Town

Savannah

Gulf of Mexico

D Most city-dwellers were Loyalists, but rural Patriots were more numerous. As British control increased, more colonists spoke out against British taxes and refused to buy taxed goods.

The Rebellion Builds

Loyalties of Colonists, 1775

- Patriot (for independence)
- Loyalist (for Britain)
- Neutral (no strong opinion)
- Patriot action
- British action

4 The British defeat Patriots waiting at Lexington.

3 Patriot messengers race west to warn of British troops.

Concord

Concord R.

Prescott

Mystic River

Lexington

Medford

Winnisimmet

5 Patriots defeat British, forcing them back to Boston.

Menotomy (Arlington)

Revere

Charlestown

Sudbury River

1 Patriot guns and gunpowder are stored at Concord.

Waltham

Charles River

Boston

Boston Harbor

Dawes

Newton

2 British troops march toward Concord to capture Patriot weapons.

MASSACHUSETTS

E In 1775 Patriots fought back when British troops tried to capture Patriot weapons stored near Boston. The battles at Lexington and Concord began the Revolutionary War.

Lexington and Concord
April 18–19, 1775

- Patriot messengers (Revere, Dawes, and Prescott)
- Patriot troops (Minutemen)
- British troops
- Patriot victory
- British victory

0   4   8 miles

0   4   8 kilometers

1776
The Declaration of Independence proclaims that the colonies are no longer under British rule.

Where was the Revolutionary War fought?

The quest for independence led rebel colonists, called Patriots, into war with Great Britain's professional army.

▶ The British had better-trained and better-equipped soldiers.

▶ Patriots fought on familiar land and had support from France and other European nations.

▶ After more than six years of fighting, British troops surrendered to the Patriots in 1781.

▶ The colonists officially won their independence with the signing of the Treaty of Paris in 1783.

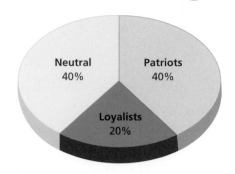

A **Taking Sides**

Loyalists supported the British government and did not want independence. Even more colonists were neutral and did not take either side.

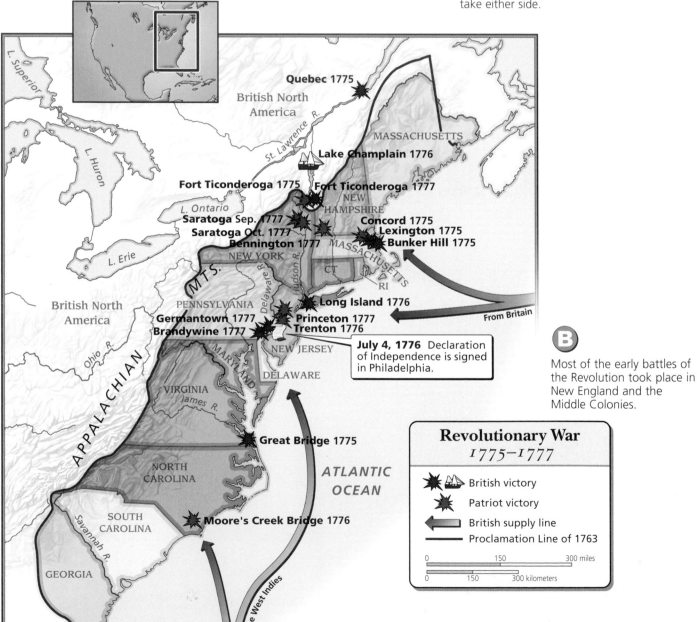

July 4, 1776 Declaration of Independence is signed in Philadelphia.

B

Most of the early battles of the Revolution took place in New England and the Middle Colonies.

Revolutionary War
1775–1777

✹⛵	British victory
✹	Patriot victory
⬅	British supply line
—	Proclamation Line of 1763

0   150   300 miles
0   150   300 kilometers

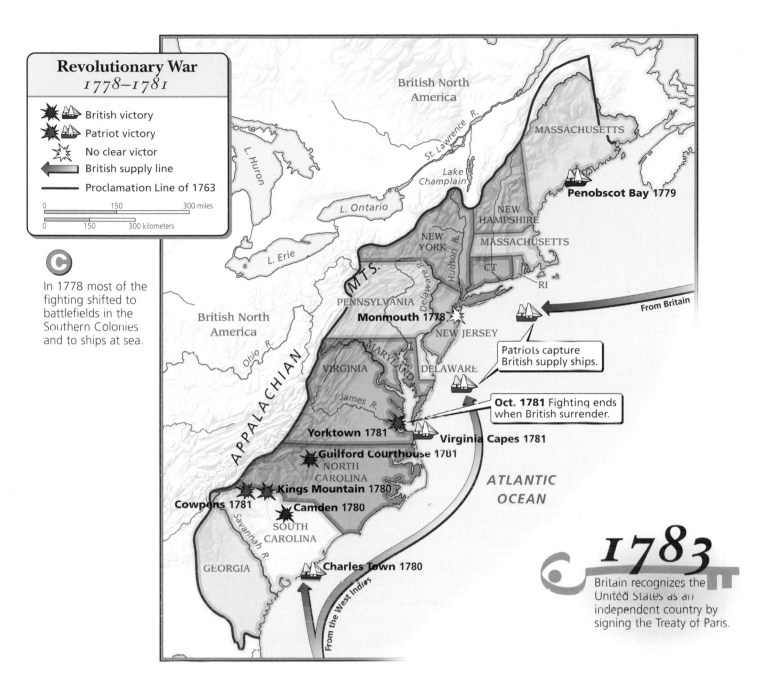

Revolutionary War
1778–1781

- ![British victory] British victory
- ![Patriot victory] Patriot victory
- ![No clear victor] No clear victor
- ← British supply line
- — Proclamation Line of 1763

0 — 150 — 300 miles
0 — 150 — 300 kilometers

British North America

MASSACHUSETTS

 Penobscot Bay 1779

NEW HAMPSHIRE

NEW YORK

MASSACHUSETTS

CT

RI

PENNSYLVANIA

Monmouth 1778

From Britain

NEW JERSEY

British North America

Patriots capture British supply ships.

VIRGINIA

MARYLAND

DELAWARE

James R.

Oct. 1781 Fighting ends when British surrender.

Yorktown 1781

Virginia Capes 1781

Guilford Courthouse 1781

NORTH CAROLINA

ATLANTIC OCEAN

Kings Mountain 1780

Cowpens 1781

Camden 1780

SOUTH CAROLINA

Charles Town 1780

GEORGIA

From the West Indies

L. Huron

L. Ontario

L. Erie

St. Lawrence R.

Lake Champlain

Ohio R.

APPALACHIAN MTS.

Delaware R.

Hudson R.

Savannah R.

C

In 1778 most of the fighting shifted to battlefields in the Southern Colonies and to ships at sea.

1783

Britain recognizes the United States as an independent country by signing the Treaty of Paris.

D

George Washington commanded the Patriots and their French allies in the final defeat of the British at Yorktown.

British 10,000

Patriots 25,700

E ## Soldiers' Deaths

The human cost of the Revolutionary War was high. Patriot soldiers who died during the war outnumbered the population of Philadelphia.

How did the United States get its start?

In 1776, one year after the Revolutionary War began, the colonies became the United States of America. But the new country did not yet have a government.

▶ After the war, the United States gained land previously claimed by the British and long held by Native Americans.

▶ In 1787 the new U.S. Constitution defined the nation's government and laws.

▶ The Constitution had to be approved, or *ratified*, by nine states before the first presidential election could take place.

Indian Lands
1775

CHOCTAW Indian nation

☐ Indian lands lost by 1775

▨ Remaining Indian lands

—— Colonial boundary

A When the Revolution began, Native Americans held nearly all land west of the colonies. Battles during the war and settlement afterward forced many Indians farther west.

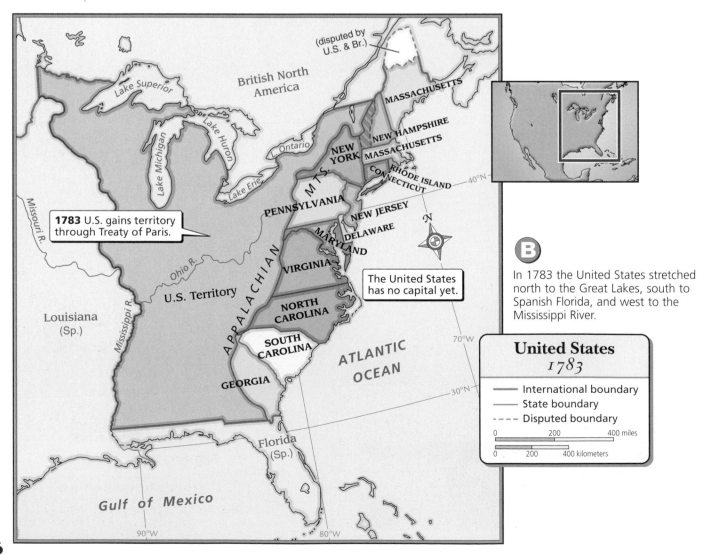

1783 U.S. gains territory through Treaty of Paris.

The United States has no capital yet.

B In 1783 the United States stretched north to the Great Lakes, south to Spanish Florida, and west to the Mississippi River.

United States
1783

——— International boundary

—— State boundary

- - - Disputed boundary

0   200   400 miles

0   200   400 kilometers

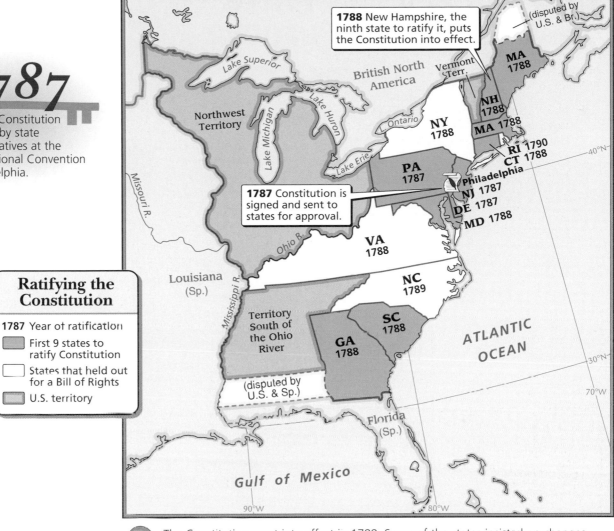

1787

The U.S. Constitution is signed by state representatives at the Constitutional Convention in Philadelphia.

1788 New Hampshire, the ninth state to ratify it, puts the Constitution into effect.

1787 Constitution is signed and sent to states for approval.

British North America

Northwest Territory

Lake Superior

Lake Michigan

Lake Huron

Lake Erie

Lake Ontario

Vermont Terr.

(disputed by U.S. & Br.)

MA 1788

NH 1788

NY 1788

MA 1788

RI 1790

CT 1788

Philadelphia

PA 1787

NJ 1787

DE 1787

MD 1788

VA 1788

NC 1789

SC 1788

GA 1788

Missouri R.

Ohio R.

Mississippi R.

Louisiana (Sp.)

Territory South of the Ohio River

(disputed by U.S. & Sp.)

Florida (Sp.)

ATLANTIC OCEAN

Gulf of Mexico

40°N

30°N

70°W

80°W

90°W

Ratifying the Constitution

1787 Year of ratification

First 9 states to ratify Constitution

States that held out for a Bill of Rights

U.S. territory

C

George Washington, the victorious general from the Revolutionary War, was a signer of the U.S. Constitution. Two years later he became the first President of the United States.

D The Constitution went into effect in 1788. Some of the states insisted on changes protecting the rights of the people. These changes, the *Bill of Rights*, were added to the Constitution in 1791.

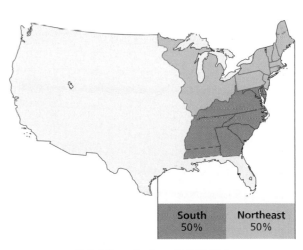

| South 50% | Northeast 50% |

Total Population: 3,929,214

E **U.S. Population by Region,** *1790*

No region dominated the United States in 1790. The numbers of people living in the Northeast and in the South were nearly identical.

How did settlers move west in the late 1700s?

In the late 1700s, Americans began settling on land west of the Appalachian Mountains.

► In 1775 Daniel Boone cleared a path called the Wilderness Road, the first wagon trail across the Appalachians.

► Soon afterward, thousands of Americans settled in Kentucky and Tennessee.

► Many pioneers also settled in the Northwest Territory and the new Mississippi Territory.

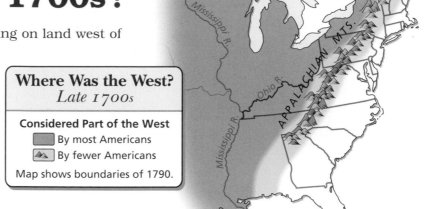

Where Was the West?
Late 1700s

Considered Part of the West
By most Americans
By fewer Americans
Map shows boundaries of 1790.

A To most Americans of the late 1700s, "the West" was no longer the Appalachians. It now extended from west of the mountains to the Mississippi River and beyond.

B Only a few rough roads and trails, or *traces*, crossed the rugged Appalachians and the Indian homelands in river valleys farther west. Settlers needed weeks to make the trip.

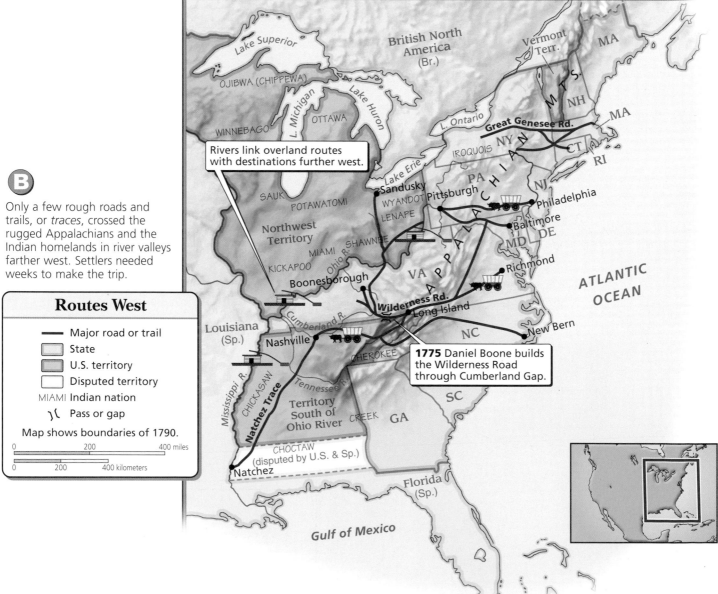

Rivers link overland routes with destinations further west.

1775 Daniel Boone builds the Wilderness Road through Cumberland Gap.

Routes West

― Major road or trail
▢ State
▢ U.S. territory
▢ Disputed territory
MIAMI Indian nation
)(Pass or gap

Map shows boundaries of 1790.

0   200   400 miles
0   200   400 kilometers

C Pioneers had to build their homes, clear forests for farmland, and grow their food. Oxen like these, at a restored pioneer site, provided the muscle power needed to haul heavy loads.

United States
1800

— International boundary
— State boundary
- - - Territorial or disputed boundary
✪ National capital

D By 1800 enough pioneers had moved west to create two new states: Kentucky and Tennessee. Both settlers and Native Americans lived in the new U.S. states and territories.

1792
Kentucky becomes the first U.S. state west of the Appalachians.

British North America

L. Superior

L. Michigan

L. Huron

L. Ontario

L. Erie

(disputed by U.S. & Br.)

MASSACHUSETTS
VERMONT

NEW HAMPSHIRE

NEW YORK

MASSACHUSETTS

RHODE ISLAND

CONNECTICUT

40°N

PENNSYLVANIA

NEW JERSEY

Indiana Territory

Northwest Terr.

Washington, D.C.

DELAWARE

MARYLAND

VIRGINIA

1800 The new capital of the United States is Washington, D.C.

KENTUCKY

Louisiana (Fr.)

NORTH CAROLINA

TENNESSEE

SOUTH CAROLINA

Terr. South of Ohio River

GEORGIA

30°N

Mississippi Terr.

New Spain

Florida (Sp.)

ATLANTIC OCEAN

Gulf of Mexico

90°W

80°W

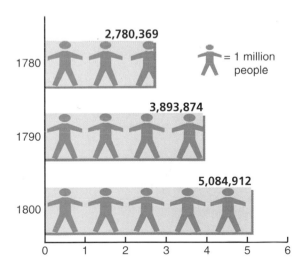

Year	Population	
1780	2,780,369	🚶 = 1 million people
1790	3,893,874	
1800	5,084,912	

0 1 2 3 4 5 6

E **U.S. Population, 1780–1800**

The population nearly doubled in just 20 years. The growing population quickly filled new territories.

How did growth change the United States?

Between 1790 and 1830, the United States gained 11 new states. Three distinct regions developed during this period.

▶ The North, with its growing number of textile mills, became America's first industrial region.

▶ The South become a wealthy agricultural region with cash crops like cotton.

▶ The Old Northwest became an important food supplier for the other two regions.

▶ The three regions began to depend on each other for goods that were not produced locally.

A In 1800 most Americans were farmers. The first settlers west of the Appalachians were able to raise only enough food for their own families.

B "Mill girls" were among the first American factory workers. Most came from farm families and hoped to put aside some money before they married.

1793

Eli Whitney invents the cotton gin, which helps increase cotton production in the South.

1790 First U.S. textile mill opens.

Map labels

(disputed by U.S. & Br.)

British North America

Lake Superior

Mississippi R.

L. Huron

Lake Michigan

L. Ontario

L. Erie

NH

MA

NY VT

MA
Boston

Northwest Territory

New York City
PA
NJ
CT RI
Philadelphia
MD
DE

40°N

Indiana Territory

Ohio R.

VA

KY

APPALACHIAN MTS.

NC

70°W

Louisiana (Fr.)

Mississippi R.

TN

SC

Territory South of Ohio River

GA
Charleston

New Spain

Mississippi Terr.

30°N

Florida (Sp.)

ATLANTIC OCEAN

Gulf of Mexico

90°W

80°W

Land Use
1800

☐ Settled area

▦ Manufacturing center

Farming

🐄 Beef 🐖 Pork

🌽 Corn 🌿 Rice

☁ Cotton 🍃 Tobacco

🐄 Dairy 🌾 Wheat

0   200   400 miles

0   200   400 kilometers

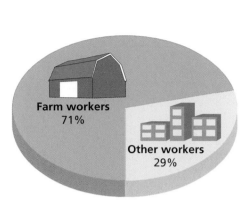

C Labor Force, *1830*

By 1830 nearly three of every ten American workers earned a living in factories and at other jobs away from the farm.

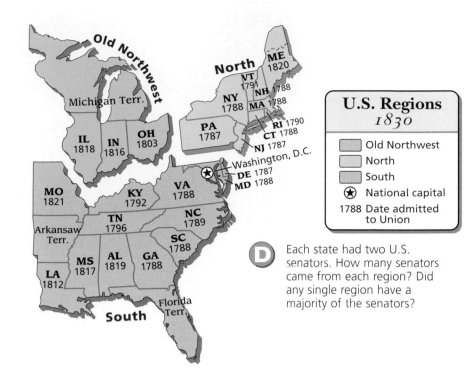

U.S. Regions
1830

- Old Northwest
- North
- South
- ⊛ National capital
- 1788 Date admitted to Union

D Each state had two U.S. senators. How many senators came from each region? Did any single region have a majority of the senators?

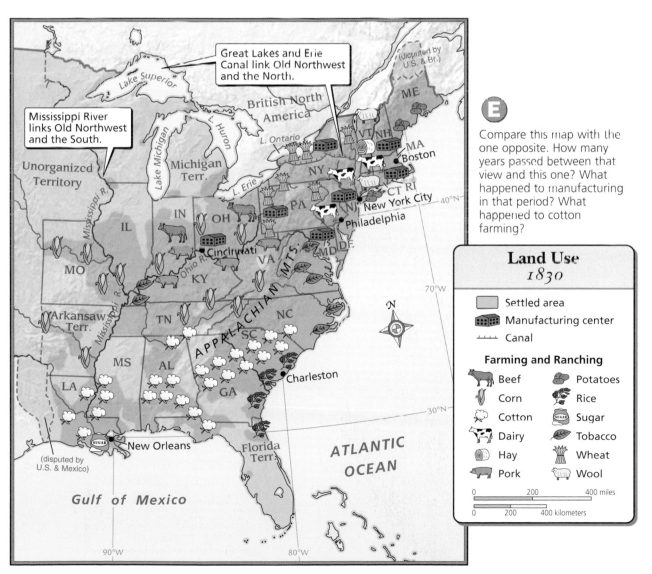

Great Lakes and Erie Canal link Old Northwest and the North.

Mississippi River links Old Northwest and the South.

E Compare this map with the one opposite. How many years passed between that view and this one? What happened to manufacturing in that period? What happened to cotton farming?

Land Use
1830

- Settled area
- Manufacturing center
- Canal

Farming and Ranching

- Beef
- Corn
- Cotton
- Dairy
- Hay
- Pork
- Potatoes
- Rice
- Sugar
- Tobacco
- Wheat
- Wool

0 200 400 miles
0 200 400 kilometers

Who explored the Far West?

During the early 1800s, the United States gained new lands west of the Mississippi River. The largest was the vast Louisiana Purchase of 1803.

▶ The next year Meriwether Lewis and William Clark began exploring the northern part of the new U.S. territory.

▶ Mountain men and U.S. army officers explored other western lands in the early 1800s.

▶ The American explorers discovered that many Indian nations already lived in the West.

Louisiana Purchase

▨	United States in 1802
▧	Louisiana Purchase, 1803
⋯⋯	State boundary today

A The Louisiana Purchase gave the United States control over the Mississippi River and territory that extended west to the Rocky Mountains.

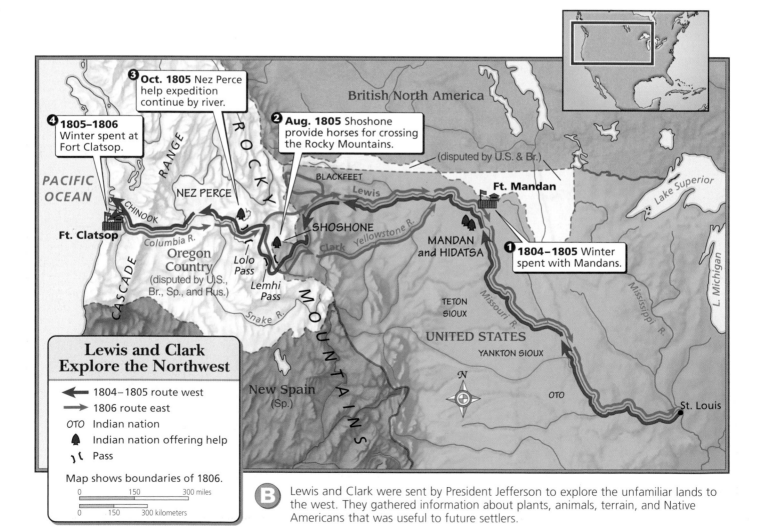

③ Oct. 1805 Nez Perce help expedition continue by river.

④ 1805–1806 Winter spent at Fort Clatsop.

② Aug. 1805 Shoshone provide horses for crossing the Rocky Mountains.

① 1804–1805 Winter spent with Mandans.

Lewis and Clark Explore the Northwest

◀━	1804–1805 route west
━▶	1806 route east
OTO	Indian nation
♠	Indian nation offering help
⟨	Pass

Map shows boundaries of 1806.

0   150   300 miles

0   150   300 kilometers

B Lewis and Clark were sent by President Jefferson to explore the unfamiliar lands to the west. They gathered information about plants, animals, terrain, and Native Americans that was useful to future settlers.

C Many Indian nations provided help to the U.S. explorers crossing their lands. Others fought the intruders, such as these Blackfeet along Lewis and Clark's route across Montana.

1803

The United States doubles its size by purchasing the Louisiana Territory from France.

D Major Stephen Long and others prepared detailed maps for the U.S. Army. Like other mountain men who explored the West, Jedediah Smith was a fur trader.

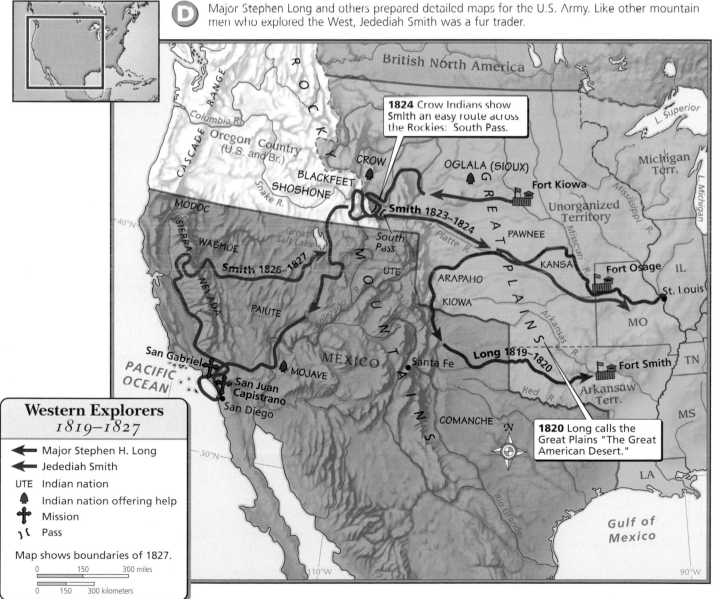

British North America

ROCKY

Columbia R.

CASCADE RANGE

Oregon Country (U.S. and Br.)

BLACKFEET
SHOSHONE

Snake R.

1824 Crow Indians show Smith an easy route across the Rockies: South Pass.

CROW

OGLALA (SIOUX)

L. Superior

Fort Kiowa

Michigan Terr.

L. Michigan

Smith 1823–1824

Unorganized Territory

Mississippi R.

MODOC

40°N

Great Salt Lake

South Pass

N. Platte R.

PAWNEE

G R E A T

Missouri R.

SIERRA

WASHOE

UTE

KANSA

Fort Osage

IL

NEVADA

Smith 1826–1827

ARAPAHO

P L A I N S

St. Louis

PAIUTE

Colorado R.

M O U N T A I N S

KIOWA

Arkansas R.

MO

San Gabriel

PACIFIC OCEAN

MEXICO

MOJAVE

Santa Fe

Long 1819–1820

Fort Smith

TN

San Juan Capistrano

San Diego

Red R.

Arkansaw Terr.

MS

COMANCHE

N

1820 Long calls the Great Plains "The Great American Desert."

LA

Rio Grande

Gulf of Mexico

Western Explorers
1819–1827

⬅ Major Stephen H. Long

⬅ Jedediah Smith

UTE — Indian nation

🔱 Indian nation offering help

✝ Mission

)(Pass

Map shows boundaries of 1827.

0   150   300 miles

0   150   300 kilometers

30°N

110°W

90°W

43

How did ways of travel change?

In the 1800s, roads often were muddy and full of ruts. Waterways and railroads were the main travel routes.

▶ Steamboats—the first boats with engines—made travel faster than ever before.

▶ Canals linked natural waterways and allowed boats to reach new places.

▶ Railroads brought direct routes and greater speed. Rivers and canals froze, but railroads ran all year long.

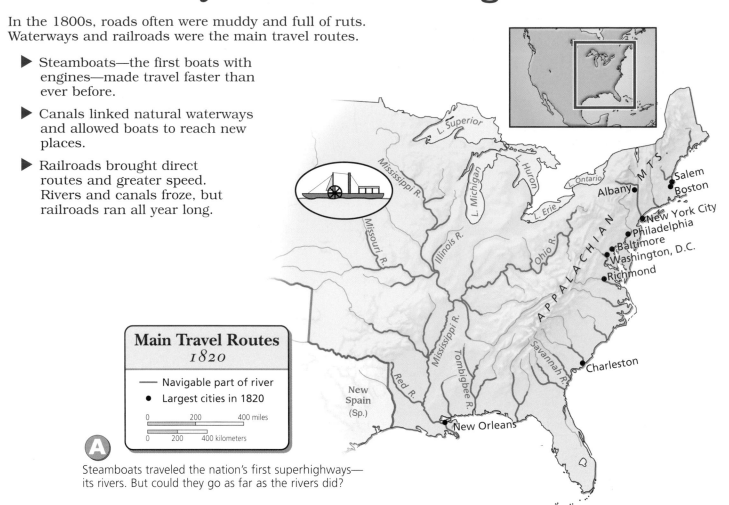

Main Travel Routes
1820

—— Navigable part of river
● Largest cities in 1820

0   200   400 miles
0   200   400 kilometers

A Steamboats traveled the nation's first superhighways— its rivers. But could they go as far as the rivers did?

1825

The Erie Canal opens, linking the Hudson River in the Northeast with the Great Lakes in the Old Northwest.

B Canal boats were towed by horses walking along the water. Most canals were too shallow for steamboats.

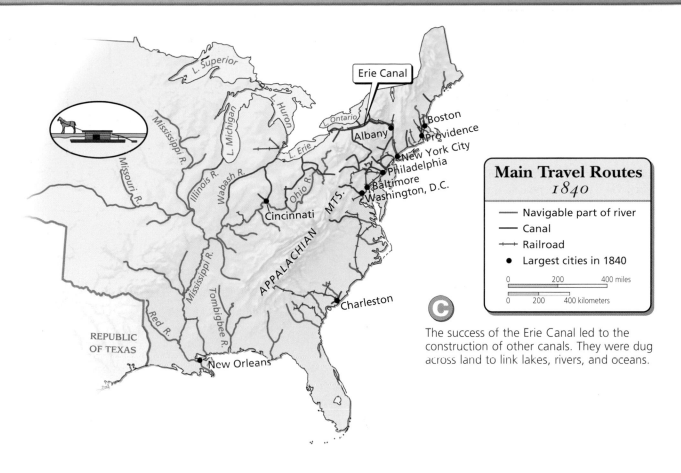

Main Travel Routes
1840

— Navigable part of river
— Canal
—+— Railroad
● Largest cities in 1840

0 — 200 — 400 miles
0 — 200 — 400 kilometers

C The success of the Erie Canal led to the construction of other canals. They were dug across land to link lakes, rivers, and oceans.

D Miles of U.S. Railroad Track

Between 1840 and 1860, railroad construction boomed in the East. How many more miles of rail were there in 1860 than in 1840?

1840 ▦ 2,818 miles

1860 ▦▦▦▦▦▦▦▦▦▦▦ 30,626 miles

E Trains traveled faster than canal boats or steamboats. Railroads could be built almost anywhere, through mountains or far from natural waterways.

Main Travel Routes
1860

— Navigable part of river
— Canal
—+— Railroad
● Largest cities in 1860

0 — 200 — 400 miles
0 — 200 — 400 kilometers

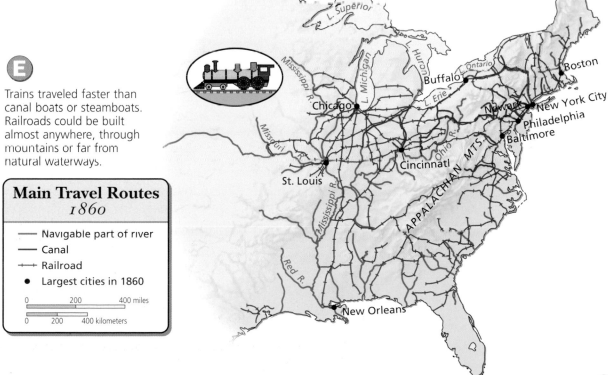

How did the United States grow in the mid-1800s?

In the mid-1800s, the U.S. population grew rapidly, and so did the demand for new lands.

▶ The government seized Indian lands east of the Mississippi River and then sold them to white settlers.

▶ Americans began settling in Texas, still part of Mexico. By 1836 there were so many of them there that they formed the independent Republic of Texas.

▶ The United States gained even more land after a treaty with Britain and the War with Mexico.

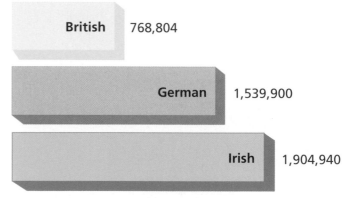

British	768,804
German	1,539,900
Irish	1,904,940

Total immigrants: 4,933,912*
*Includes groups not shown.

A **Largest Immigrant Groups,** *1830–1860*

Immigration helped our country's population grow quickly. Compare this graph with the map on page 23. Which were the largest immigrant groups in colonial times?

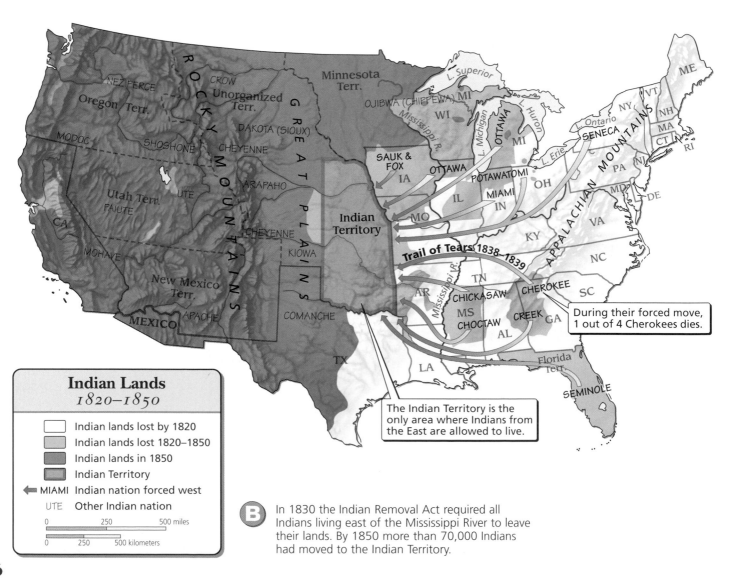

During their forced move, 1 out of 4 Cherokees dies.

The Indian Territory is the only area where Indians from the East are allowed to live.

Indian Lands
1820–1850

☐ Indian lands lost by 1820
▨ Indian lands lost 1820–1850
▨ Indian lands in 1850
▨ Indian Territory
← MIAMI Indian nation forced west
UTE Other Indian nation

0   250   500 miles
0   250   500 kilometers

B In 1830 the Indian Removal Act required all Indians living east of the Mississippi River to leave their lands. By 1850 more than 70,000 Indians had moved to the Indian Territory.

When Americans formed the Republic of Texas, thousands of Mexicans still lived there. Today roughly 3 of every 10 Texans are of Mexican descent.

1845

Texas becomes the 28th state in the United States.

D In just eight years, the size of the United States grew by two-thirds. Some land was gained through war, and some by agreement or by purchase.

American Expansion
1845–1853

How Land Was Gained

🏺 Agreement

💰 Purchase

⚙ War

1845 Year land was gained

Map shows boundaries of today.

British North America

U.S. and Britain agree to split Oregon at 49°N.

Oregon Country
1846

Mexico loses war with U.S., gives up its northern lands.

Mexican Cession
1848

UNITED STATES
(before 1845)

Republic of Texas accepts offer from U.S. Congress to be added to the United States.

L. Superior

L. Michigan

L. Huron

L. Erie

L. Ontario

40°N

ATLANTIC OCEAN

Gadsden Purchase
1853

U.S. buys Mexican land for a southern railroad route.

Texas Annexation
1845

30°N

30°N

120°W

PACIFIC OCEAN

MEXICO

Gulf of Mexico

N

80°W

90°W

Why did Americans move to the Far West?

In the mid-1800s, thousands of Americans crossed the Great Plains and the Rocky Mountains and settled in the Far West.

► Pioneer families in covered wagons headed for the rich farmland available in the Oregon Territory.

► Mormons, who were attacked for their religious beliefs, moved to the unsettled Utah Territory.

► Adventurers flocked to California in search of gold.

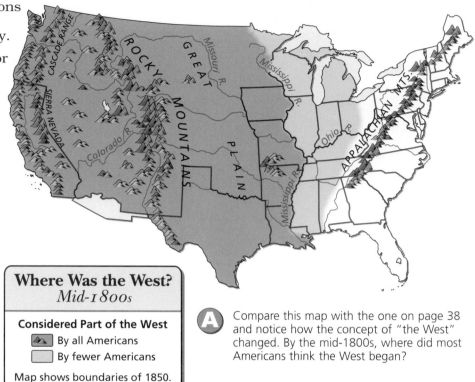

1848

Gold is discovered in California. Thousands stampede to the new territory.

Where Was the West?
Mid-1800s

Considered Part of the West
- By all Americans
- By fewer Americans

Map shows boundaries of 1850.

(A) Compare this map with the one on page 38 and notice how the concept of "the West" changed. By the mid-1800s, where did most Americans think the West began?

(B) Children traveled the Oregon Trail with their families. Some pioneers walked beside the family wagon the entire way—almost 2,000 miles.

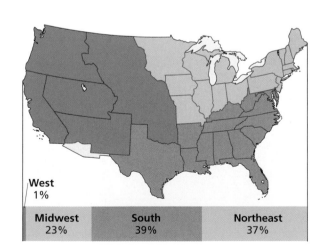

West 1%			
Midwest 23%	South 39%		Northeast 37%

Total population: 23,054,152

(C) **U.S. Population by Region, *1850***

Compare this graph with the graph on page 37. Most U.S. residents in the West in 1850 moved there after 1840.

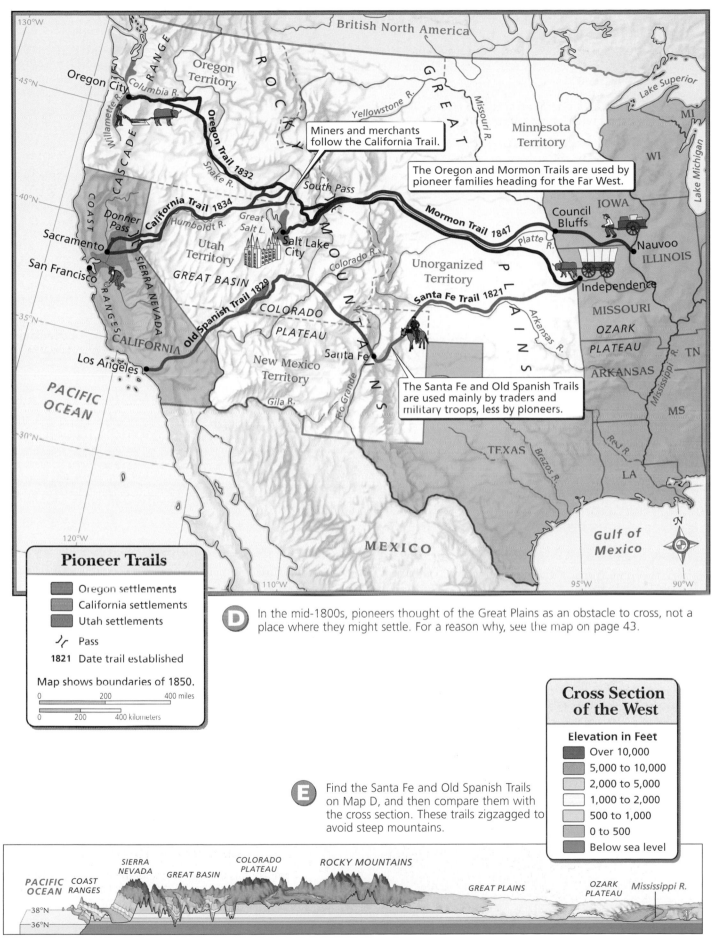

British North America

Oregon Territory

Minnesota Territory

Oregon City

Columbia R.

Yellowstone R.

Missouri R.

Lake Superior

MI

WI

Oregon Trail 1832

Snake R.

South Pass

Miners and merchants follow the California Trail.

The Oregon and Mormon Trails are used by pioneer families heading for the Far West.

Lake Michigan

California Trail 1834

Donner Pass

Sacramento

San Francisco

Humboldt R.

Great Salt L.

Salt Lake City

Utah Territory

GREAT BASIN

Mormon Trail 1847

Council Bluffs

Platte R.

IOWA

Nauvoo

ILLINOIS

Colorado R.

Unorganized Territory

Independence

MISSOURI

Old Spanish Trail 1829

COLORADO PLATEAU

Santa Fe Trail 1821

Arkansas R.

OZARK PLATEAU

TN

Los Angeles

New Mexico Territory

Santa Fe

Gila R.

Rio Grande

The Santa Fe and Old Spanish Trails are used mainly by traders and military troops, less by pioneers.

ARKANSAS

MS

PACIFIC OCEAN

CALIFORNIA

COAST RANGES

SIERRA NEVADA

CASCADE RANGE

ROCKY MOUNTAINS

GREAT PLAINS

Red R.

Mississippi R.

TEXAS

Brazos R.

LA

MEXICO

Gulf of Mexico

Pioneer Trails

- Oregon settlements
- California settlements
- Utah settlements
-)(Pass
- **1821** Date trail established

Map shows boundaries of 1850.

0   200   400 miles

0   200   400 kilometers

D In the mid-1800s, pioneers thought of the Great Plains as an obstacle to cross, not a place where they might settle. For a reason why, see the map on page 43.

Cross Section of the West

Elevation in Feet

- Over 10,000
- 5,000 to 10,000
- 2,000 to 5,000
- 1,000 to 2,000
- 500 to 1,000
- 0 to 500
- Below sea level

E Find the Santa Fe and Old Spanish Trails on Map D, and then compare them with the cross section. These trails zigzagged to avoid steep mountains.

PACIFIC OCEAN

COAST RANGES

SIERRA NEVADA

GREAT BASIN

COLORADO PLATEAU

ROCKY MOUNTAINS

GREAT PLAINS

OZARK PLATEAU

Mississippi R.

38°N

36°N

How did slavery divide the nation?

The Southern economy depended on slavery. To ensure that slavery continued, the South had to have political power.

▶ The wealth of the South came from cash crops harvested with slave labor.

▶ There was more manufacturing in the North, but some of it depended on raw materials from the South.

▶ The South wanted slavery to be allowed in new states and territories.

▶ The North feared it soon would be outvoted in the Senate if slavery spread.

SOUTH
Total population: 12 million

Free 66%
Slaves 34%

NORTH AND WEST
Total population: 19 million

Free 99%
Slaves 1%

Ⓐ **Slavery and Freedom,** *1860*

All Southern states allowed slavery, but it was banned in all Northern and Western states except Missouri.

Ⓑ

The South wanted a balance of power in the Senate. The North wanted to keep slavery from spreading. The Missouri Compromise, passed by Congress, did both.

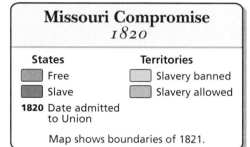

Missouri Compromise
1820

States	Territories
▢ Free	▢ Slavery banned
▢ Slave	▢ Slavery allowed

1820 Date admitted to Union

Map shows boundaries of 1821.

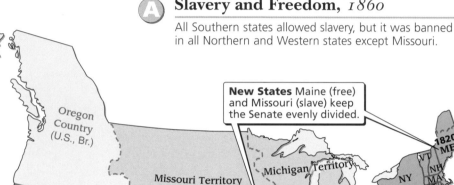

New States Maine (free) and Missouri (slave) keep the Senate evenly divided.

Territories Slavery banned north of 36°30'.

Oregon Country (U.S., Br.)

Missouri Territory

Michigan Territory

1820 ME
VT NH
NY MA CT RI
PA NJ DE
IL IN OH MD
VA
1821 MO KY
TN NC
Arkansaw Territory SC
MS AL GA
LA
Florida Territory

MEXICO

Ⓒ

The Supreme Court decided that a slave named Dred Scott could not sue to become free. The decision allowed slavery in every territory.

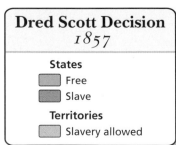

Dred Scott Decision
1857

States
▢ Free
▢ Slave

Territories
▢ Slavery allowed

Washington Terr.
Oregon Terr.
Minnesota Territory
Nebraska Territory
ME
VT NH
NY MA CT RI
WI MI
Utah Territory
IA
PA NJ DE
IL IN OH MD
Kansas Terr.
CA
MO
KY VA
New Mexico Territory
Unorganized Terr.
AR
TN NC
SC
TX
MS AL GA
LA
FL

D Abolitionists helped slaves escape with the *Underground Railroad*, a system of secret paths and hiding places.

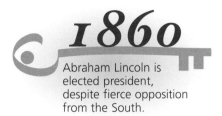

1860

Abraham Lincoln is elected president, despite fierce opposition from the South.

E Cotton plantations, which depended on slave labor, formed the "Cotton Belt" of the South. Northern textile mills depended on Southern cotton.

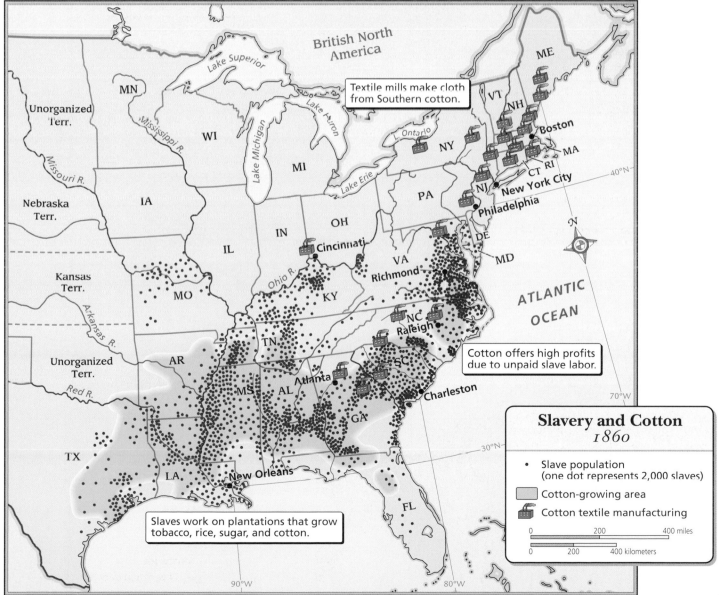

Textile mills make cloth from Southern cotton.

Cotton offers high profits due to unpaid slave labor.

Slaves work on plantations that grow tobacco, rice, sugar, and cotton.

British North America

Lake Superior

MN

Unorganized Terr.

WI

Lake Michigan

Lake Huron

MI

L. Ontario

Lake Erie

NY

ME

VT

NH

Boston

MA

CT RI

NJ

New York City

Philadelphia

PA

DE

MD

40°N

Missouri R.

Mississippi R.

Nebraska Terr.

IA

IL

IN

OH

Cincinnati

Ohio R.

VA

Richmond

ATLANTIC OCEAN

Kansas Terr.

MO

KY

TN

NC

Raleigh

SC

Unorganized Terr.

AR

Arkansas R.

Red R.

MS

AL

Atlanta

GA

Charleston

70°W

TX

LA

New Orleans

30°N

FL

Slavery and Cotton
1860

• Slave population (one dot represents 2,000 slaves)

▨ Cotton-growing area

⛏ Cotton textile manufacturing

0   200   400 miles

0   200   400 kilometers

90°W

80°W

Where were early Civil War battles fought?

Soon after Lincoln was elected, 11 Southern states withdrew, or *seceded*, from the United States. This act led to the Civil War.

▶ The states that seceded formed the Confederate States of America, or *Confederacy*.

▶ The remaining states fought to preserve an undivided United States, the *Union*.

▶ The Union set up a blockade to stop trade and deprive the Confederacy of resources.

▶ Although outnumbered, the Confederate army won most major battles in the first years of the war.

1861

Eleven states secede from the Union to form the Confederacy.

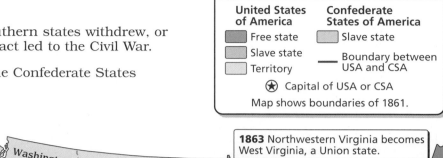

The Union and the Confederacy

United States of America
- Free state
- Slave state
- Territory

Confederate States of America
- Slave state
- Boundary between USA and CSA

⭐ Capital of USA or CSA

Map shows boundaries of 1861.

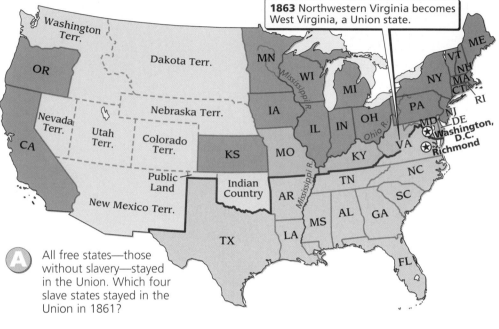

1863 Northwestern Virginia becomes West Virginia, a Union state.

A All free states—those without slavery—stayed in the Union. Which four slave states stayed in the Union in 1861?

B Confederate troops wore gray. Most came from Confederate states, but some came from Union states too.

C Union troops wore blue. Most were white Northerners, but there also were many free blacks and ex-slaves.

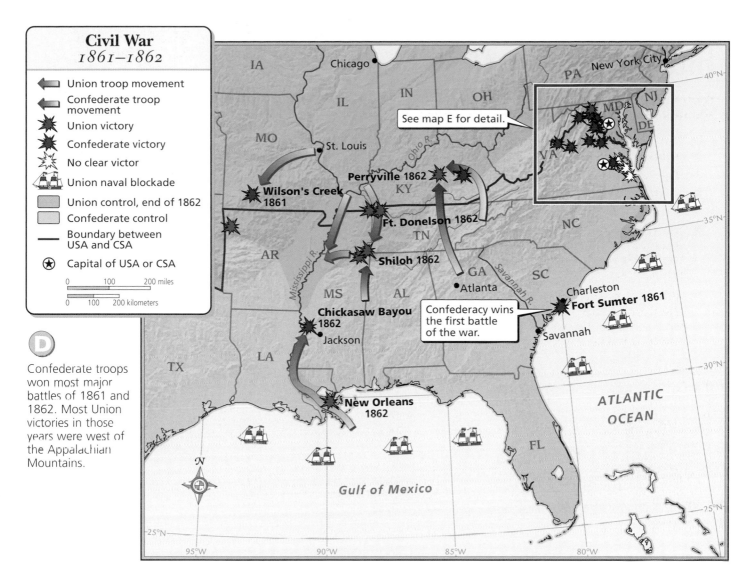

Civil War
1861–1862

Legend:
- Union troop movement
- Confederate troop movement
- Union victory
- Confederate victory
- No clear victor
- Union naval blockade
- Union control, end of 1862
- Confederate control
- Boundary between USA and CSA
- Capital of USA or CSA

0   100   200 miles
0   100   200 kilometers

See map E for detail.

Perryville 1862
Wilson's Creek 1861
Ft. Donelson 1862
Shiloh 1862
Chickasaw Bayou 1862
New Orleans 1862
Fort Sumter 1861

Confederacy wins the first battle of the war.

IA, Chicago, New York City, PA, IN, OH, IL, MO, St. Louis, KY, TN, NC, MD, NJ, DE, VA, AR, MS, AL, GA, Atlanta, SC, Charleston, Savannah, LA, TX, Jackson, FL, ATLANTIC OCEAN, Gulf of Mexico

Mississippi R., Ohio R., Savannah R.

D Confederate troops won most major battles of 1861 and 1862. Most Union victories in those years were west of the Appalachian Mountains.

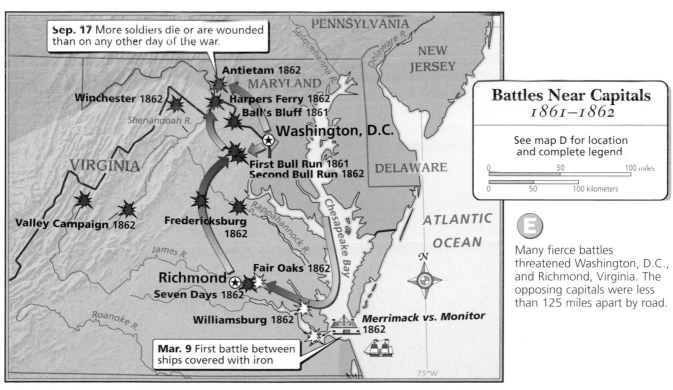

Sep. 17 More soldiers die or are wounded than on any other day of the war.

Antietam 1862
Winchester 1862
Harpers Ferry 1862
Ball's Bluff 1861
Washington, D.C.
First Bull Run 1861
Second Bull Run 1862
Valley Campaign 1862
Fredericksburg 1862
Fair Oaks 1862
Richmond
Seven Days 1862
Williamsburg 1862
Merrimack vs. Monitor 1862

PENNSYLVANIA, MARYLAND, NEW JERSEY, VIRGINIA, DELAWARE, ATLANTIC OCEAN

Shenandoah R., Susquehanna R., Delaware R., Rappahannock R., Chesapeake Bay, James R., Roanoke R.

Mar. 9 First battle between ships covered with iron

Battles Near Capitals
1861–1862

See map D for location and complete legend.

0   50   100 miles
0   50   100 kilometers

E Many fierce battles threatened Washington, D.C., and Richmond, Virginia. The opposing capitals were less than 125 miles apart by road.

Where were later Civil War battles fought?

The Union had the advantage of more people and greater resources. In the last years of the war, it gained control over more and more of the Confederacy.

▶ Major Union victories split the Confederacy in 1863 and again in 1864.

▶ The bloody fighting claimed hundreds of thousands of lives on both sides.

▶ After the war, new amendments to the Constitution abolished slavery and gave citizenship rights to former slaves.

A Southern cities like Richmond had to be rebuilt after the war. Most Civil War battles were fought in Confederate states.

B Which victories gave the Union control of the Mississippi River? Which began and ended the March to the Sea?

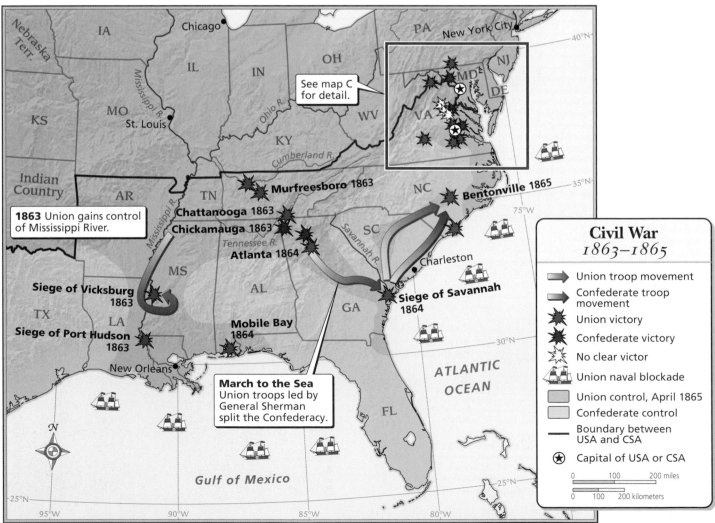

1863 Union gains control of Mississippi River.

March to the Sea
Union troops led by General Sherman split the Confederacy.

Murfreesboro 1863
Chattanooga 1863
Chickamauga 1863
Atlanta 1864
Bentonville 1865
Siege of Vicksburg 1863
Siege of Port Hudson 1863
Mobile Bay 1864
Siege of Savannah 1864
New Orleans
St. Louis
Chicago
New York City
Charleston

Civil War
1863–1865

→ Union troop movement
→ Confederate troop movement
✦ Union victory
✦ Confederate victory
✦ No clear victor
⛵ Union naval blockade
▢ Union control, April 1865
▢ Confederate control
— Boundary between USA and CSA
✪ Capital of USA or CSA

0   100   200 miles
0   100   200 kilometers

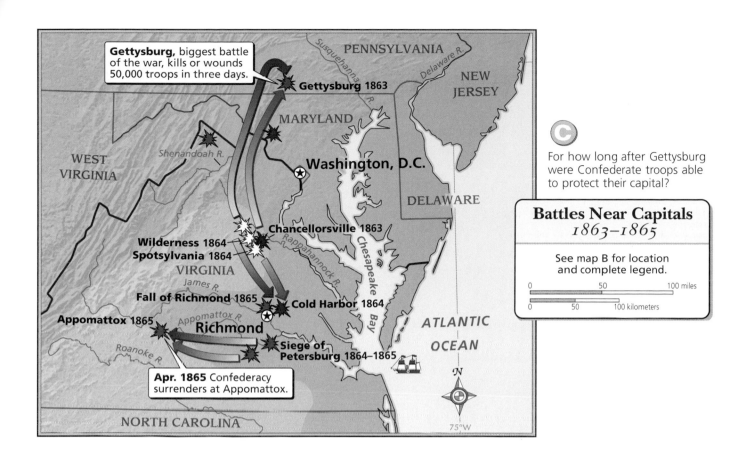

Gettysburg, biggest battle of the war, kills or wounds 50,000 troops in three days.

PENNSYLVANIA

Gettysburg 1863

NEW JERSEY

MARYLAND

WEST VIRGINIA

Shenandoah R.

Washington, D.C.

DELAWARE

Chancellorsville 1863

Wilderness 1864
Spotsylvania 1864

VIRGINIA

James R.

Fall of Richmond 1865

Cold Harbor 1864

Chesapeake Bay

Appomattox 1865

Appomattox R.

Richmond

Siege of Petersburg 1864–1865

ATLANTIC OCEAN

Roanoke R.

Apr. 1865 Confederacy surrenders at Appomattox.

NORTH CAROLINA

75°W

C

For how long after Gettysburg were Confederate troops able to protect their capital?

Battles Near Capitals
1863–1865

See map B for location and complete legend.

| 0 | 50 | 100 miles |
| 0 | 50 | 100 kilometers |

1865
The Confederacy surrenders and slavery is abolished

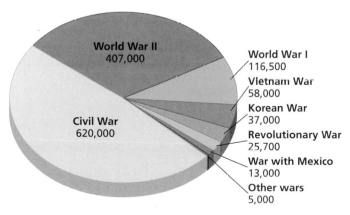

World War II
407,000

World War I
116,500

Vietnam War
58,000

Korean War
37,000

Revolutionary War
25,700

Civil War
620,000

War with Mexico
13,000

Other wars
5,000

D **American War Deaths,** *1775–2000*

Nearly as many American troops died in the Civil War as in all other wars combined. Many died on the battlefield, but many others died later, from loss of blood or infection or disease.

E After the war, Southern blacks continued working on plantations in exchange for housing and supplies. But this system, called *sharecropping*, kept them in debt.

How did railroads change the West?

Railroads spread across the West after the Civil War, replacing the rough trails used by wagons and stagecoaches.

▶ Railroads made it practical for ranchers to send cattle to market in distant parts of the country.

▶ Farmers bought Western land from railroad companies. Later they sent their crops East by train.

▶ Merchants moved West too and built new towns.

▶ Trains carried minerals from mines in Western mountains to factories in Eastern cities.

1869

The first transcontinental railroad is completed, linking the populous East with the distant West Coast.

1870	52,922 miles
1890	166,703 miles

A **Miles of U.S. Railroad Track**

Compare this graph with the one on page 45. After the Civil War, the growing East got additional railroads while the West got railroads for the first time.

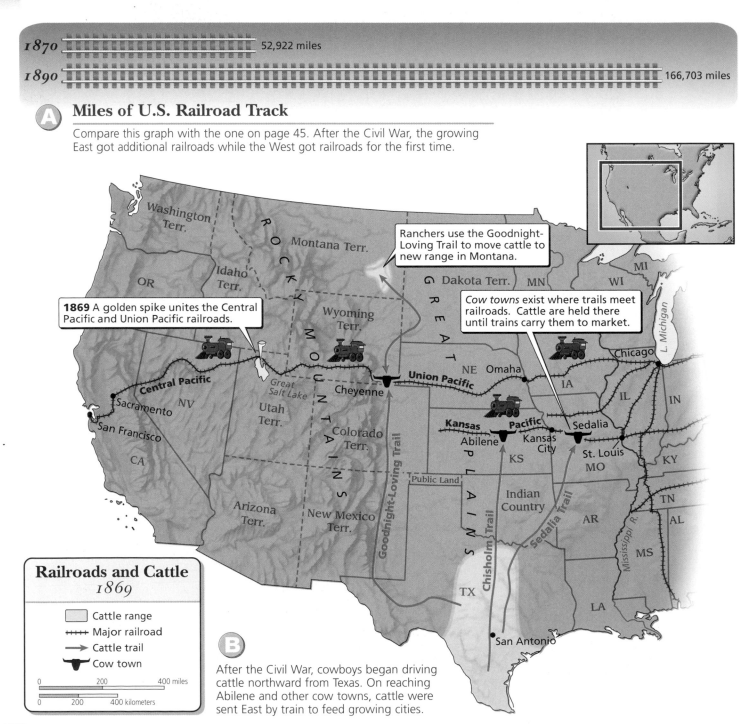

Ranchers use the Goodnight-Loving Trail to move cattle to new range in Montana.

1869 A golden spike unites the Central Pacific and Union Pacific railroads.

Cow towns exist where trails meet railroads. Cattle are held there until trains carry them to market.

Railroads and Cattle
1869

- ▢ Cattle range
- ┼┼┼┼ Major railroad
- → Cattle trail
- 🐂 Cow town

0   200   400 miles
0   200   400 kilometers

B After the Civil War, cowboys began driving cattle northward from Texas. On reaching Abilene and other cow towns, cattle were sent East by train to feed growing cities.

C Some railroad companies offered cheap land and free transportation to people willing to settle near their railroads. But limited water made the Great Plains hard to farm.

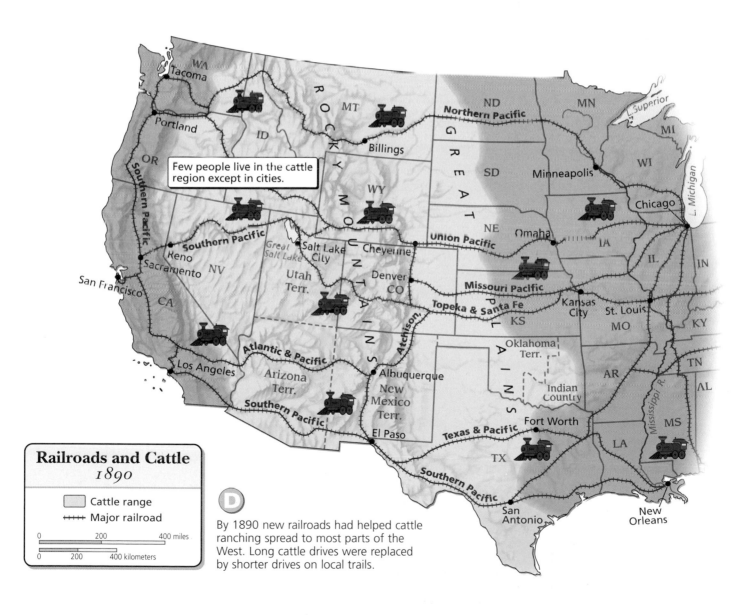

Few people live in the cattle region except in cities.

Railroads and Cattle
1890

- Cattle range
- +++++ Major railroad

0 ___ 200 ___ 400 miles
0 ___ 200 ___ 400 kilometers

D By 1890 new railroads had helped cattle ranching spread to most parts of the West. Long cattle drives were replaced by shorter drives on local trails.

How did the lives of Indians change in the late 1800s?

After the Civil War, miners and settlers moved west with the protection of U.S. troops. Indians fought unsuccessfully to keep their lands.

▶ Between 1860 and 1890, the Western Indians lost 25 percent of their population—mostly from diseases brought by white people, but also in battles with U.S. troops.

▶ They also lost 90 percent of their lands, and what was left became government reservations.

▶ White hunters killed nearly all 15 million buffalo on the Great Plains, and the Plains Indians lost their main source of food.

A In 1860 most Plains Indian children did not attend school. Instead they learned skills from adults in their villages.

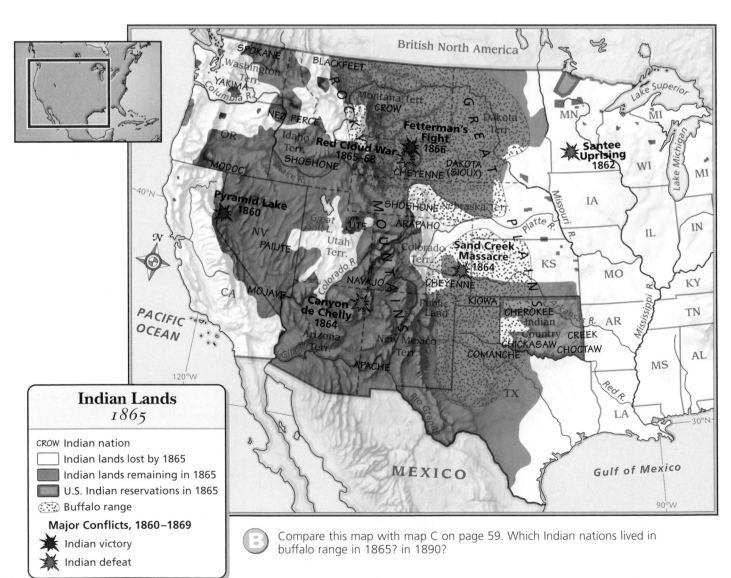

Indian Lands
1865

CROW Indian nation
☐ Indian lands lost by 1865
◼ Indian lands remaining in 1865
◼ U.S. Indian reservations in 1865
⬚ Buffalo range
Major Conflicts, 1860–1869
✦ Indian victory
✦ Indian defeat

B Compare this map with map C on page 59. Which Indian nations lived in buffalo range in 1865? in 1890?

Compare the maps on these pages with the similar maps on pages 9, 36, and 46. What happened to Indian lands between 1492 and 1890?

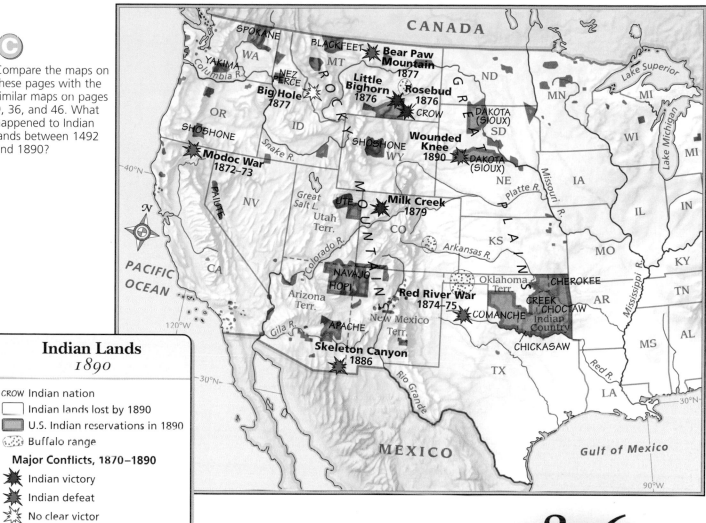

Indian Lands
1890

CROW Indian nation

☐ Indian lands lost by 1890

▨ U.S. Indian reservations in 1890

⬚ Buffalo range

Major Conflicts, 1870–1890

✸ Indian victory

✸ Indian defeat

✸ No clear victor

By 1890 many Indian children were being sent to boarding schools. There they had to give up traditional Indian names and ways of life.

1876

Dakota and Cheyenne warriors overwhelm U.S. troops at the Battle of Little Bighorn, also known as Custer's Last Stand.

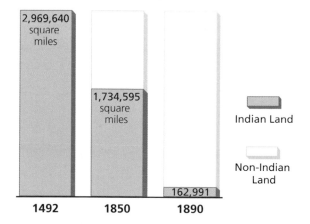

2,969,640 square miles

1,734,595 square miles

162,991

1492   1850   1890

Indian Land

Non-Indian Land

Shrinking Indian Lands

How much land did Indians lose in the 358 years between 1492 and 1850? How much in the 40 years that followed?

How did a growing population change U.S. industry?

In the late 1800s, a growing population, vast natural resources, and new inventions helped U.S. industry grow.

▶ The U.S. population more than doubled between 1860 and 1900.

▶ New ranchers and farmers provided food for growing cities.

▶ Miners provided minerals for new factories.

▶ Immigrants, former farm workers, and children filled many of the new factory jobs.

▶ Factories turned new inventions into products that changed the way Americans lived.

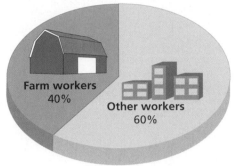

Ⓐ Labor Force, *1900*

New kinds of farm equipment made it possible to grow more food with fewer workers. Compare this graph with the one on page 41.

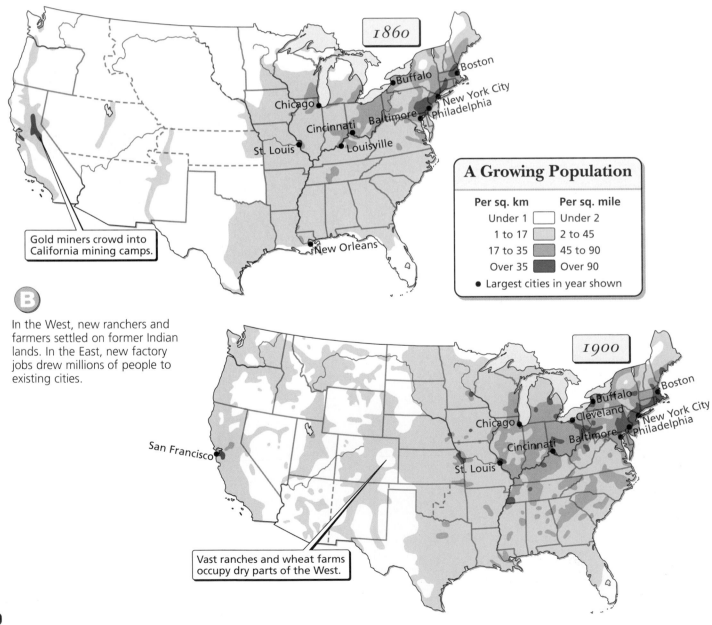

Gold miners crowd into California mining camps.

Ⓑ

In the West, new ranchers and farmers settled on former Indian lands. In the East, new factory jobs drew millions of people to existing cities.

A Growing Population

Per sq. km		Per sq. mile
Under 1	☐	Under 2
1 to 17	▨	2 to 45
17 to 35	▨	45 to 90
Over 35	■	Over 90
● Largest cities in year shown		

Vast ranches and wheat farms occupy dry parts of the West.

C In the 1800s, few laws limited child labor. Many children worked 10 hours a day, 6 days a week, to help their families.

1896

Henry Ford builds his first automobile in Detroit, Michigan.

D Where was steel made in 1900? Where did factories use steel to make other products? To see why meat products came from Kansas City and Chicago, refer to map D on page 57.

1900 The United States leads the world in steel production.

Major Industrial Products
1900

● Major manufacturing center

New Devices
- Cameras
- Electric lighting
- Sewing machines
- Typewriters

Basic Goods
- Cloth
- Flour
- Meat products

Vehicles
- Automobiles
- Farm equipment
- Locomotives
- Pullman railroad cars

Fuel and Metals
- Refined oil
- Steel
- Other metals

How did immigration and war change the United States?

In the late 1800s and early 1900s, new immigrants and foreign wars made the United States more aware of the outside world.

▶ Earlier most immigrants were Northern and Western Europeans. Now vast numbers were coming from Southern and Eastern Europe.

▶ In a war with Spain, the United States won new territories and world recognition. It also gained other territories in more peaceful ways.

▶ After the United States helped the Allies win World War I, it was seen as a true world power.

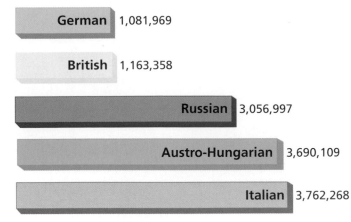

German 1,081,969

British 1,163,358

Russian 3,056,997

Austro-Hungarian 3,690,109

Italian 3,762,268

Total immigrants: 18,102,930*
*Includes groups not shown.

 Largest Immigrant Groups, *1890 to 1918*

Immigrants from Southern and Eastern Europe spoke languages and practiced religions that were unfamiliar to most Americans. Compare this graph with the one on page 46.

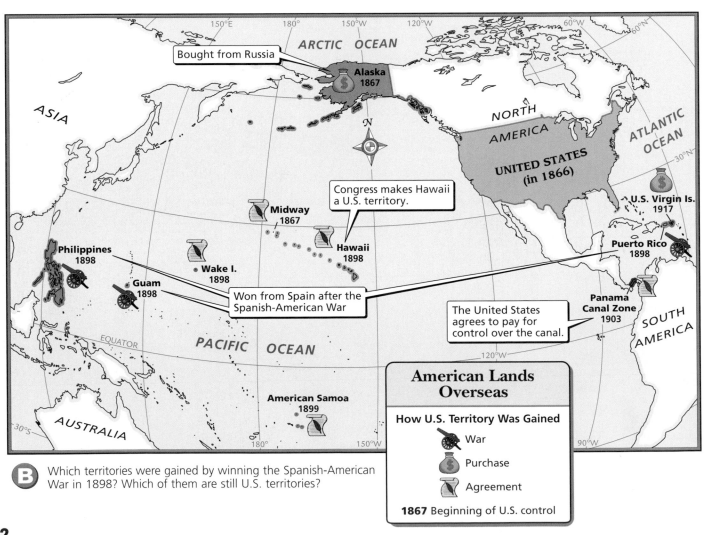

Bought from Russia

Alaska 1867

Midway 1867

Congress makes Hawaii a U.S. territory.

Philippines 1898

Wake I. 1898

Guam 1898

Hawaii 1898

Won from Spain after the Spanish-American War

American Samoa 1899

UNITED STATES (in 1866)

U.S. Virgin Is. 1917

Puerto Rico 1898

The United States agrees to pay for control over the canal.

Panama Canal Zone 1903

American Lands Overseas

How U.S. Territory Was Gained

🔫 War

💰 Purchase

📜 Agreement

1867 Beginning of U.S. control

B Which territories were gained by winning the Spanish-American War in 1898? Which of them are still U.S. territories?

C After 1892 nearly all immigrants from Europe had to pass an inspection at Ellis Island in New York City before they were allowed to enter the United States.

1917

The United States enters World War I on the side of the Allies.

D American troops, weapons, and supplies helped the Allies defeat the Central Powers in 1918. For the first time, the United States had played a key role in world affairs.

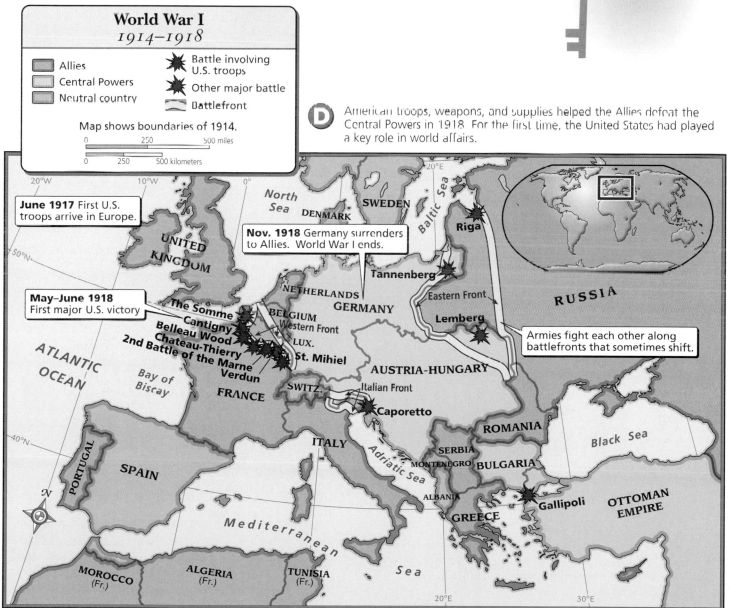

World War I
1914–1918

- Allies
- Central Powers
- Neutral country
- Battle involving U.S. troops
- Other major battle
- Battlefront

Map shows boundaries of 1914.

0   250   500 miles
0   250   500 kilometers

June 1917 First U.S. troops arrive in Europe.

Nov. 1918 Germany surrenders to Allies. World War I ends.

May–June 1918 First major U.S. victory.

Armies fight each other along battlefronts that sometimes shift.

The Somme
Cantigny
Belleau Wood
Chateau-Thierry
2nd Battle of the Marne
Verdun
St. Mihiel

Western Front
Eastern Front
Italian Front

Riga
Tannenberg
Lemberg
Caporetto
Gallipoli

UNITED KINGDOM
NETHERLANDS
BELGIUM
LUX.
GERMANY
FRANCE
SWITZ.
ITALY
SPAIN
PORTUGAL
DENMARK
SWEDEN
RUSSIA
AUSTRIA-HUNGARY
ROMANIA
SERBIA
MONTENEGRO
BULGARIA
ALBANIA
GREECE
OTTOMAN EMPIRE
MOROCCO (Fr.)
ALGERIA (Fr.)
TUNISIA (Fr.)

ATLANTIC OCEAN
North Sea
Baltic Sea
Bay of Biscay
Adriatic Sea
Black Sea
Mediterranean Sea

20°W   10°W   0°   20°E   30°E
50°N
40°N

How did America change in the early 1900s?

American society went through many changes during World War I and the decades that followed.

▶ Thousands of African Americans moved from the rural South to the urban North.

▶ The 19th Amendment gave women the right to vote.

▶ Economic prosperity followed the war, but then ended abruptly when the stock market crashed.

▶ Much of rural America finally got electrical power.

B Women fought for decades for *suffrage*, the right to vote. They won it in 1920.

A Between 1915 and 1930, nearly 500,000 African Americans moved from Southern farms to Northern cities. They hoped to find jobs and escape discrimination and poverty.

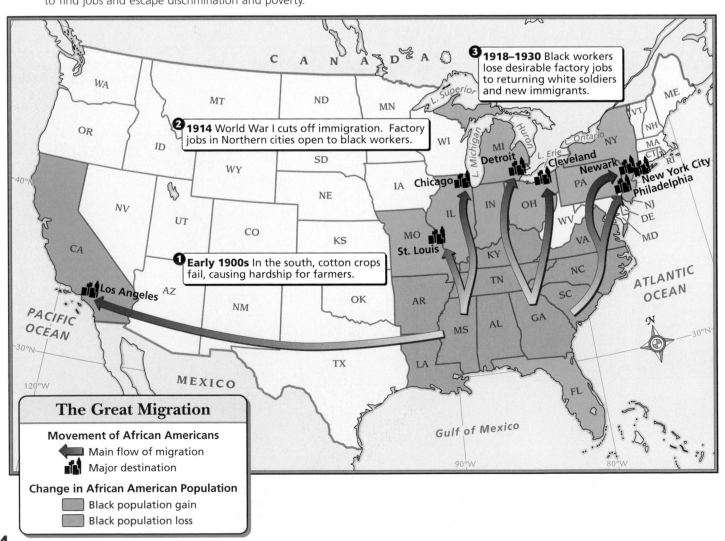

3 **1918–1930** Black workers lose desirable factory jobs to returning white soldiers and new immigrants.

2 **1914** World War I cuts off immigration. Factory jobs in Northern cities open to black workers.

1 **Early 1900s** In the south, cotton crops fail, causing hardship for farmers.

The Great Migration

Movement of African Americans
- ◀ Main flow of migration
- 🏙 Major destination

Change in African American Population
- Black population gain
- Black population loss

1929

The stock market crashes, sending the United States into the Great Depression.

C

The Great Depression was a time of economic hardship that lasted for over ten years. Many Americans lost their jobs, their savings, and even their homes.

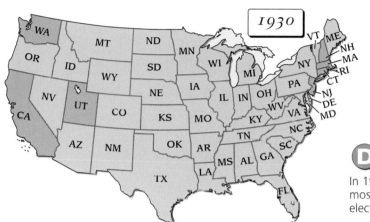

1930

D

In 1930 nearly one of every four Americans lived on farms and most farms had no electricity. Where were the farms that got electricity between 1930 and 1945?

Farms with Electricity

- Less than one-third
- One-third to two-thirds
- More than two-thirds

1945

Before
ELECTRICITY
After

E **Before and After Electricity**

Electricity dramatically changed life on the farm. Lights brightened homes, and radios provided instant access to news and entertainment.

Who fought in World War II?

World War II was fought by two groups of nations, the Axis and the Allies.

▶ The main Axis powers were Germany, Italy, and Japan. They started the war by invading neighboring countries.

▶ The main Allied powers were the United Kingdom, the Soviet Union, and the United States.

▶ The United States became a world superpower due to its central role in the Allied victory.

B Many Americans at home helped the war effort. Children helped by gathering scrap metal for use in war materials.

World War II Begins
1939–1942

▭	Axis power and occupied area
▮	Allied power
▯	Neutral power
➤	Axis expansion

Map shows boundaries of 1942.

A

Germany, with help from Italy, took control over much of Europe. Japan extended its power in East Asia and the Pacific.

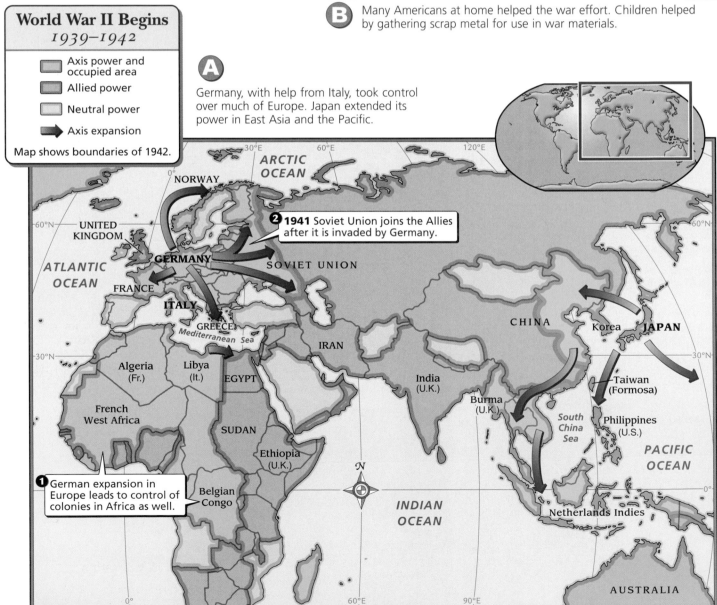

❷ **1941** Soviet Union joins the Allies after it is invaded by Germany.

❶ German expansion in Europe leads to control of colonies in Africa as well.

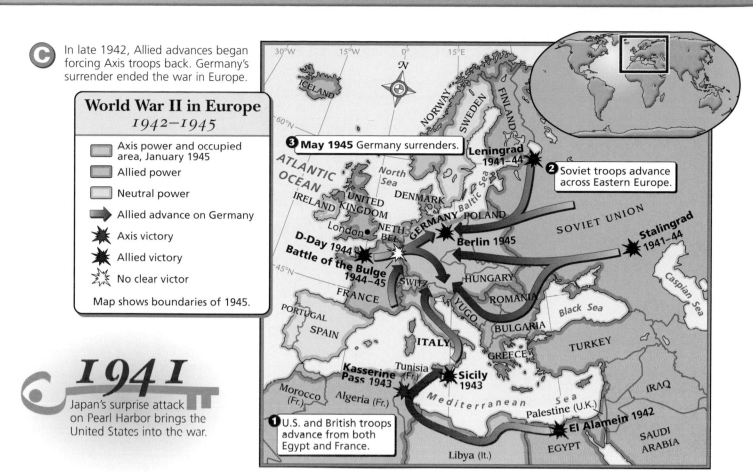

C In late 1942, Allied advances began forcing Axis troops back. Germany's surrender ended the war in Europe.

World War II in Europe
1942–1945

- Axis power and occupied area, January 1945
- Allied power
- Neutral power
- → Allied advance on Germany
- ✦ Axis victory
- ✦ Allied victory
- ✦ No clear victor

Map shows boundaries of 1945.

3 May 1945 Germany surrenders.

2 Soviet troops advance across Eastern Europe.

Leningrad 1941–44

Stalingrad 1941–44

Berlin 1945

D-Day 1944
Battle of the Bulge 1944–45

Kasserine Pass 1943

Sicily 1943

El Alamein 1942

1 U.S. and British troops advance from both Egypt and France.

1941
Japan's surprise attack on Pearl Harbor brings the United States into the war.

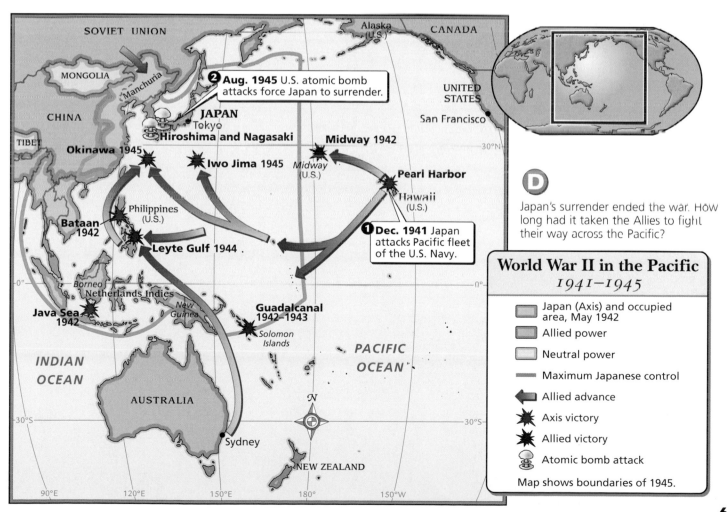

2 Aug. 1945 U.S. atomic bomb attacks force Japan to surrender.

JAPAN
Tokyo
Hiroshima and Nagasaki

Midway 1942

Okinawa 1945

Iwo Jima 1945

Pearl Harbor

Hawaii (U.S.)

Bataan 1942

Philippines (U.S.)

Leyte Gulf 1944

1 Dec. 1941 Japan attacks Pacific fleet of the U.S. Navy.

Java Sea 1942

Netherlands Indies

Guadalcanal 1942–1943

Solomon Islands

D Japan's surrender ended the war. How long had it taken the Allies to fight their way across the Pacific?

World War II in the Pacific
1941–1945

- Japan (Axis) and occupied area, May 1942
- Allied power
- Neutral power
- — Maximum Japanese control
- → Allied advance
- ✦ Axis victory
- ✦ Allied victory
- ☁ Atomic bomb attack

Map shows boundaries of 1945.

Where did the Cold War turn hot?

After World War II, the Communist and anti-Communist nations of the world opposed each other in what came to be called the *Cold War*.

▶ The Cold War was a political and economic struggle, but it erupted into regional shooting wars.

▶ The opposing sides were led by two superpowers, the democratic United States and the Communist Soviet Union.

▶ The threat of their nuclear weapons helped prevent a hot war between the superpowers.

▶ When the Soviet Union broke apart in 1991, the Cold War ended.

1949
The North Atlantic Treaty Organization (NATO) is formed to defend Europe from possible Communist attacks.

Communist   Anti-Communist   Neutral
✴ Regional war

A Use the map above to place the other maps in a global setting. The red symbols mark regional shooting wars besides those in Vietnam and Korea.

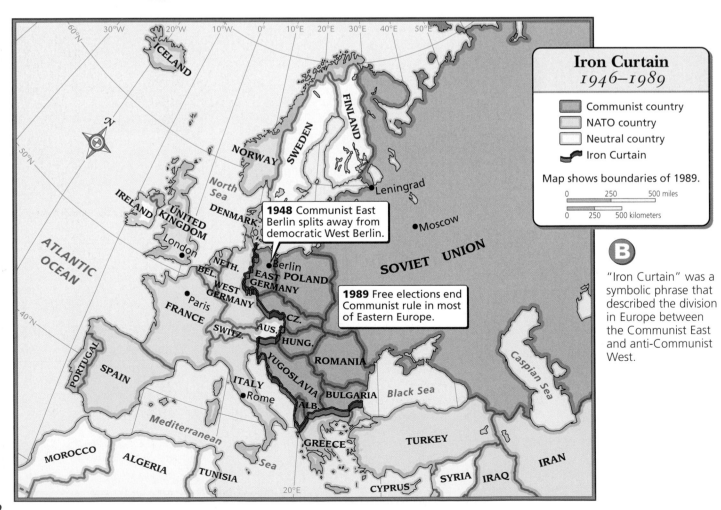

Iron Curtain
1946–1989

Communist country
NATO country
Neutral country
Iron Curtain

Map shows boundaries of 1989.

0   250   500 miles
0   250   500 kilometers

1948 Communist East Berlin splits away from democratic West Berlin.

1989 Free elections end Communist rule in most of Eastern Europe.

B "Iron Curtain" was a symbolic phrase that described the division in Europe between the Communist East and anti-Communist West.

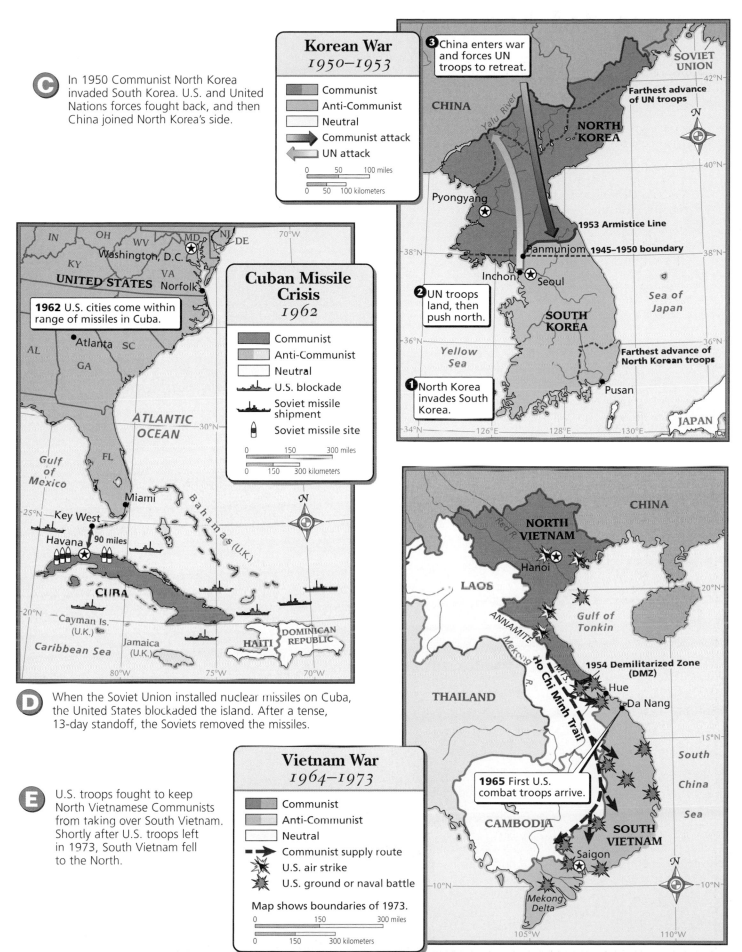

C In 1950 Communist North Korea invaded South Korea. U.S. and United Nations forces fought back, and then China joined North Korea's side.

Korean War
1950–1953

	Communist
	Anti-Communist
	Neutral
→	Communist attack
→	UN attack

0   50   100 miles
0   50   100 kilometers

❸ China enters war and forces UN troops to retreat.

SOVIET UNION

CHINA

Yalu River

Farthest advance of UN troops

NORTH KOREA

Pyongyang ★

1953 Armistice Line

Panmunjom   1945–1950 boundary

Inchon ★ Seoul

❷ UN troops land, then push north.

SOUTH KOREA

Sea of Japan

Yellow Sea

Farthest advance of North Korean troops

❶ North Korea invades South Korea.

Pusan

JAPAN

Cuban Missile Crisis
1962

1962 U.S. cities come within range of missiles in Cuba.

	Communist
	Anti-Communist
	Neutral
	U.S. blockade
	Soviet missile shipment
	Soviet missile site

0   150   300 miles
0   150   300 kilometers

IN   OH   MD   NJ   DE

WV   70°W

Washington, D.C. ★

KY

UNITED STATES   VA   Norfolk

Atlanta

AL   SC

GA

ATLANTIC OCEAN   30°N

FL

Gulf of Mexico

Miami

Key West   25°N

Havana ★   90 miles

Bahamas (U.K.)

CUBA   20°N

Cayman Is. (U.K.)

Jamaica (U.K.)

Caribbean Sea

HAITI   DOMINICAN REPUBLIC

80°W   75°W   70°W

D When the Soviet Union installed nuclear missiles on Cuba, the United States blockaded the island. After a tense, 13-day standoff, the Soviets removed the missiles.

E U.S. troops fought to keep North Vietnamese Communists from taking over South Vietnam. Shortly after U.S. troops left in 1973, South Vietnam fell to the North.

Vietnam War
1964–1973

	Communist
	Anti-Communist
	Neutral
⇢	Communist supply route
✳	U.S. air strike
✴	U.S. ground or naval battle

Map shows boundaries of 1973.

0   150   300 miles
0   150   300 kilometers

CHINA

NORTH VIETNAM

Red R.

Hanoi ★

LAOS

Gulf of Tonkin

ANNAMITE

Mekong R.

Ho Chi Minh Trail

1954 Demilitarized Zone (DMZ)

MTS.

Hue

Da Nang

1965 First U.S. combat troops arrive.

THAILAND

15°N

South China Sea

CAMBODIA

SOUTH VIETNAM

Saigon

Mekong Delta

10°N

105°W   110°W

69

Where did struggles for equal rights occur?

In the 1950s, the struggle by many Americans for respect and equal rights began to succeed.

▶ African Americans demanded that civil rights not be denied because of race.

▶ Native Americans worked to regain Indian lands and fishing rights that were protected by treaty.

▶ Mexican Americans struggled to win better farm wages and the chance to study their history in school.

▶ Women demanded, and won, equal opportunities in work and in sports.

A Some communities reacted to integration violently. Young black students, such as Ruby Bridges, needed the protection of U.S. marshals as they enrolled in formerly all-white schools.

1964

The Civil Rights Act bans racial discrimination in jobs and public places.

Indians claim the right to fish where their ancestors did.

Puyallup 1961

Mt. Rushmore 1970
Wounded Knee 1973

Traverse Bay 1973, 1979

Wareham 1996

1966 Mexican Americans form the United Farm Workers Union.

Sacramento 1966
Alcatraz I. 1969–1971
Delano 1966–1970

Denver 1969

Blue Lake 1970

1970 In nationwide protests, citizens demand that Indian treaty rights be honored.

East Los Angeles 1968

Tierra Amarilla 1967

Crystal City 1963

Mexican Americans win control of local schools for the first time.

Mexican American and Native American Protests

Mexican Americans	Native Americans
Labor dispute	Fishing rights
Land claim	Land or water claim
School dispute	Violence over claim

C Mexican American farm workers won better working conditions, and schools began to teach Mexican American history. Many Indian nations regained fishing rights in court, but few regained their former lands.

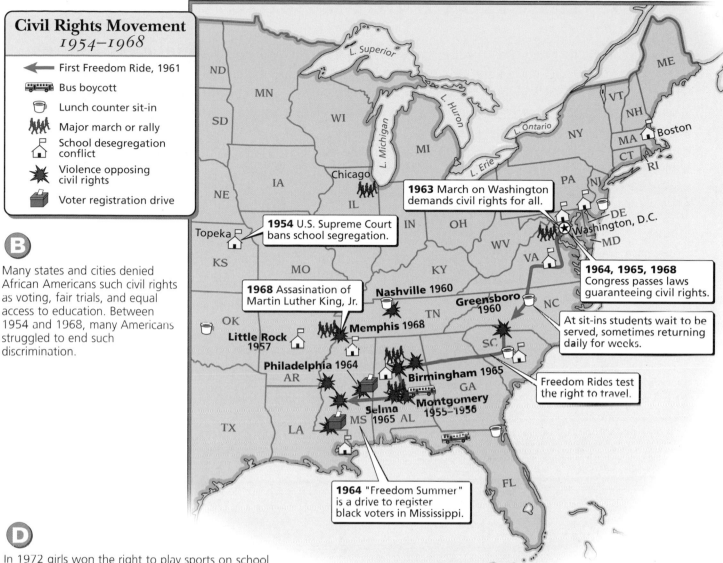

Civil Rights Movement
1954–1968

⬅ First Freedom Ride, 1961

🚌 Bus boycott

🪣 Lunch counter sit-in

👥 Major march or rally

🏠 School desegregation conflict

💥 Violence opposing civil rights

🗳 Voter registration drive

B

Many states and cities denied African Americans such civil rights as voting, fair trials, and equal access to education. Between 1954 and 1968, many Americans struggled to end such discrimination.

1954 U.S. Supreme Court bans school segregation.

1963 March on Washington demands civil rights for all.

1968 Assasination of Martin Luther King, Jr.

1964, 1965, 1968 Congress passes laws guaranteeing civil rights.

At sit-ins students wait to be served, sometimes returning daily for weeks.

Freedom Rides test the right to travel.

1964 "Freedom Summer" is a drive to register black voters in Mississippi.

Topeka • Nashville 1960 • Greensboro 1960 • Little Rock 1957 • Memphis 1968 • Philadelphia 1964 • Birmingham 1965 • Montgomery 1955–1956 • Selma 1965 • Washington, D.C. • Boston • Chicago

D

In 1972 girls won the right to play sports on school teams. Until then most schools had coaches, teams, and leagues only for boys.

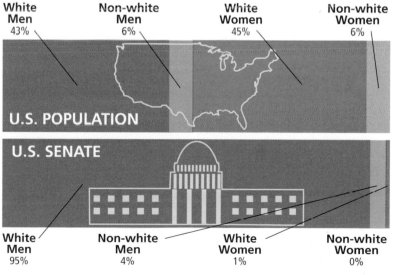

| White Men 43% | Non-white Men 6% | White Women 45% | Non-white Women 6% |

U.S. POPULATION

U.S. SENATE

| White Men 95% | Non-white Men 4% | White Women 1% | Non-white Women 0% |

E **Senators and the Public,** *1970*

In 1970, 95 percent of U.S. Senators were white men. How did the Senate differ from the population it represented?

How is America's population changing?

The population of the United States continues to grow, move, and change, just as it has throughout our country's history.

▶ The South and West have a greater share of our population than ever before.

▶ Large cities and their suburbs are homes to more and more Americans: 80.3 percent in 2000.

▶ The most recent wave of immigrants is increasing our Hispanic and Asian populations.

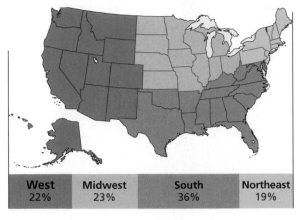

West 22%	Midwest 23%	South 36%	Northeast 19%

Total population: 281,421,906

2000

The population of the United States reaches 281,421,906 people—three times as many as in 1900.

A **U.S. Population by Region,** *2000*

Compare this graph with the graph on page 48 and the maps on page 60. New jobs in the South and West attract people to these regions.

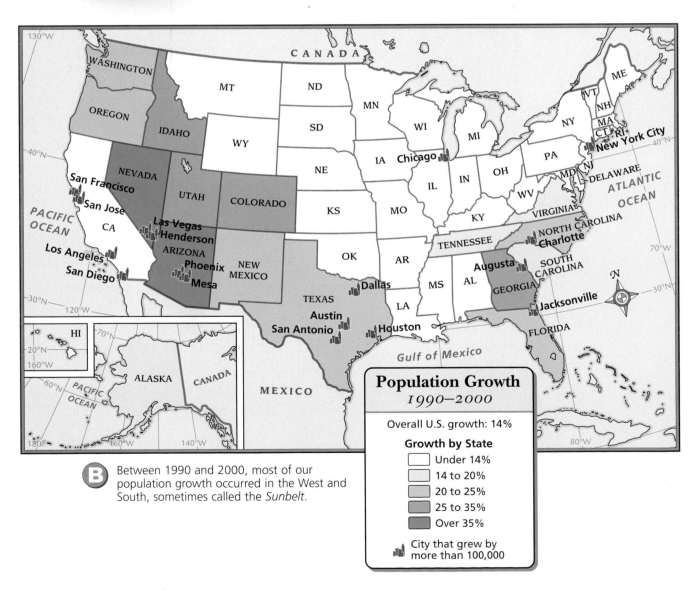

B Between 1990 and 2000, most of our population growth occurred in the West and South, sometimes called the *Sunbelt*.

Population Growth
1990–2000

Overall U.S. growth: 14%

Growth by State
- Under 14%
- 14 to 20%
- 20 to 25%
- 25 to 35%
- Over 35%

City that grew by more than 100,000

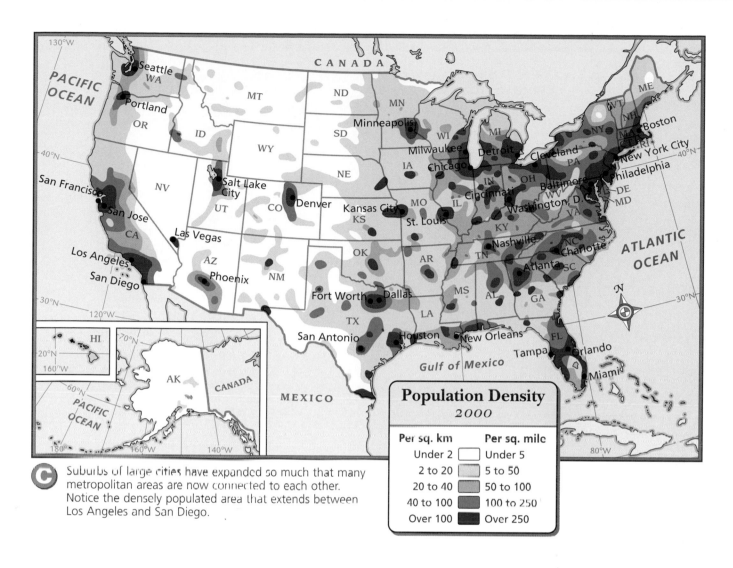

Population Density
2000

Per sq. km		Per sq. mile
Under 2		Under 5
2 to 20		5 to 50
20 to 40		50 to 100
40 to 100		100 to 250
Over 100		Over 250

C Suburbs of large cities have expanded so much that many metropolitan areas are now connected to each other. Notice the densely populated area that extends between Los Angeles and San Diego.

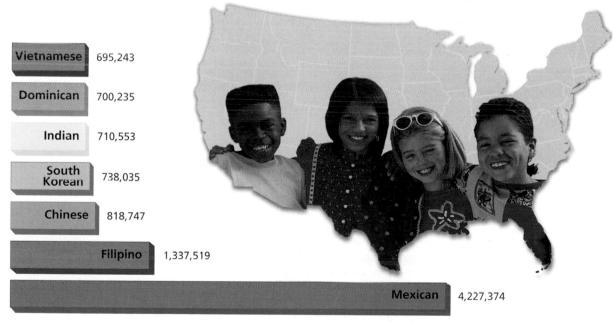

Vietnamese	695,243
Dominican	700,235
Indian	710,553
South Korean	738,035
Chinese	818,747
Filipino	1,337,519
Mexican	4,227,374

Total number of immigrants: 19,436,444*
*Includes groups not shown.

D ## Largest Immigrant Groups Since 1970

Compare this graph with the graph on page 62. Which continent did most earlier immigrants come from? Where do they come from now? Use the map on pages 80-81 to find out.

Reference Map

Physical Map
UNITED STATES

Natural Regions

Tundra or ice   Forest   Grass   Shrub or desert

〜 River and lake
▲ Mountain peak
Waterfall
Dam
Canal
Continental boundary
International boundary
State boundary

Scale
0 — 150 — 300 miles
0 — 150 — 300 kilometers

UNITED STATES

Lake Winnipeg
Lake of e Woods
Red Lake
Red R.
MINNESOTA
St. Paul
Minneapolis
Minnesota
Mississippi R.
Des Moines R.
Missouri R.
IOWA
Kansas City
Kansas R.
Flint Hills
LAHOMA
Lake O' The Cherokees
Boston Mts.
Arkansas R.
Ouachita Mts.
ARKANSAS
Lake Texoma
Dallas
Toledo Bend Res.
Sam Rayburn Res.
Brazos R.
Houston
Galveston Bay
dre I.
Gulf

Isle Royale
Mesabi Range
Lake Superior
Lake Nipigon
WISCONSIN
Wisconsin R.
Rock R.
Chicago
Illinois R.
Central Lowland
ILLINOIS
Missouri R.
MISSOURI
Lake of the Ozarks
Ozark Plateau
Table Rock Lake
KENTUCKY
Ohio River
MISSISSIPPI
Yazoo R.
Pearl R.
LOUISIANA
Mississippi River
New Orleans
Mobile Bay
Delta of the Mississippi River
Atchafalaya Bay
Red R.

Upper Peninsula
MICHIGAN
Lower Peninsula
Lake Michigan
Lake Huron
Georgian Bay
Detroit
Lake Erie
Cleveland
INDIANA
White R.
Wabash R.
OHIO
Scioto R.
WEST VIRGINIA
TENNESSEE
Memphis
Tennessee R.
Cumberland R.
Tombigbee R.
ALABAMA
Alabama R.
Chattahoochee R.
Coastal Plain
Cape San Blas
Apalachee Bay

Toronto
Lake Ontario
Niagara Falls
NEW YORK
Catskill Mts.
Pennsylvania Plateau
PENNSYLVANIA
Allegheny R.
Monongahela R.
Cumberland Plateau
Mt. Mitchell 2037 m
Appalachian
Blue Ridge
Piedmont
VIRGINIA
Roanoke R.
James R.
NORTH CAROLINA
SOUTH CAROLINA
Saluda R.
Savannah R.
Clark Hill Lake
Atlanta
GEORGIA
Pee Dee R.
Charleston
Sea Islands
Altamaha R.
FLORIDA
St. Johns R.
Cape Canaveral
Tampa Bay
Lake Okeechobee
Miami
Cape Sable

Montreal
St. Lawrence River
Moosehead Lake
MAINE
Bay of Fundy
Lake Champlain
Adirondack Mts.
Green Mts.
VERMONT
White Mts.
NEW HAMPSHIRE
Mohawk R.
Hudson R.
Boston
MASSACHUSETTS
Cape Cod
RHODE ISLAND
CONNECTICUT
New York City
Long Island
NEW JERSEY
MARYLAND
Washington, D.C.
Potomac R.
DELAWARE
Delaware Bay
Chesapeake Bay
Susquehanna R.
Albemarle Sound
Cape Hatteras
Pamlico Sound

ATLANTIC OCEAN

Gulf of Mexico

Dry Tortugas
Florida Keys
Straits of Florida

TROPIC OF CANCER
CUBA

N

95°W 90°W 85°W 80°W 75°W 70°W 65°W
45°N 40°N 35°N 30°N 25°N

Reference Map

Political Map
UNITED STATES

○○○○○○○○○	Continental boundary
▬▬▬▬▬	International boundary
▬▬▬▬▬	State boundary
⊛ **Washington, D.C.**	National capital
★ Honolulu	State capital
● **Chicago**	Large city
• Anchorage	Smaller city

Scale

0 — 150 — 300 miles

0 — 150 — 300 kilometers

Reference Map

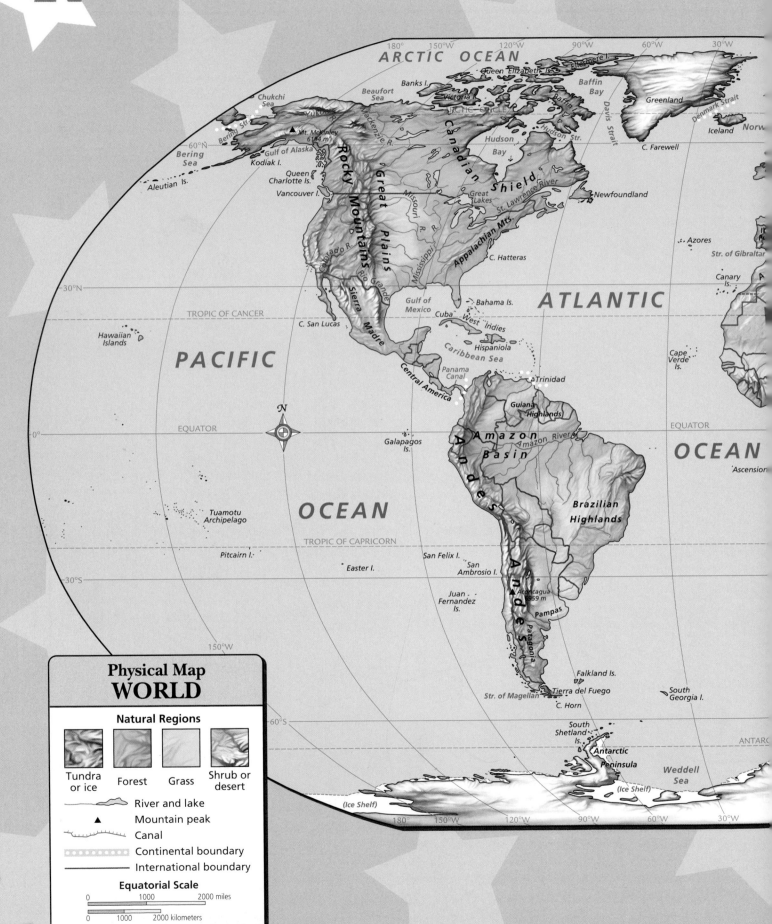

ARCTIC OCEAN

180° 150°W 120°W 90°W 60°W 30°W

Queen Elizabeth Is. Ellesmere I.

Chukchi Sea

Banks I.

Beaufort Sea

Victoria I.

Baffin Bay

Greenland

Baffin I.

Denmark Strait

Davis Strait

Iceland Norw

60°N

Bering Strait

Mt. McKinley 6194 m

Mackenzie R.

ARCTIC CIRCLE

Canadian Shield

Hudson Str.

C. Farewell

Bering Sea

Gulf of Alaska

Kodiak I.

Hudson Bay

Yukon

Rocky Mountains

Queen Charlotte Is.

Vancouver I.

Missouri R.

Great Lakes

St. Lawrence River

Newfoundland

Azores

Great Plains

Appalachian Mts.

30°N

Colorado R.

Sierra Madre

Rio Grande

Mississippi R.

C. Hatteras

Str. of Gibraltar

ATLANTIC

TROPIC OF CANCER

Canary Is.

A

C. San Lucas

Gulf of Mexico

Bahama Is.

Cuba

West Indies

Hispaniola

Hawaiian Islands

PACIFIC

Caribbean Sea

Cape Verde Is.

Central America

Panama Canal

Trinidad

N

Guiana Highlands

0°

EQUATOR

Galapagos Is.

Andes

Amazon Basin

Amazon River

EQUATOR

OCEAN

Ascension

Tuamotu Archipelago

OCEAN

Brazilian Highlands

TROPIC OF CAPRICORN

Pitcairn I.

Easter I.

San Felix I.

San Ambrosio I.

30°S

Juan Fernandez Is.

Andes

Aconcagua 6959 m

Pampas

150°W

Patagonia

Falkland Is.

South Georgia I.

Str. of Magellan

Tierra del Fuego

C. Horn

60°S

South Shetland Is.

ANTAR

Antarctic Peninsula

Weddell Sea

(Ice Shelf)

(Ice Shelf)

180° 150°W 120°W 90°W 60°W 30°W

Physical Map
WORLD

Natural Regions

Tundra or ice	Forest	Grass	Shrub or desert

River and lake

▲ Mountain peak

Canal

Continental boundary

International boundary

Equatorial Scale

0   1000   2000 miles

0   1000   2000 kilometers

ARCTIC   OCEAN

30°E   60°E   90°E   120°E   150°E   180°

Svalbard
North Cape
Scandinavian Peninsula
Novaya Zemlya
Barents Sea
Kara Sea
Severnaya Zemlya
Laptev Sea
New Siberian Is.
East Siberian Sea

Yenisey River
Central Siberian Plateau
Verkhoyansk Range
Kolyma Range
ARCTIC CIRCLE

Northern European Plain
Volga River
Ural Mountains
Ob
West Siberian Plain
Siberia
Lena River
Amur River
60°N
Kamchatka Peninsula

ALPS
Mt. Elbrus 5642 m
Caucasus Mts.
Black Sea
Aral Sea
L. Balkhash
Altai Mts.
Gobi
Manchurian Plain
Sea of Okhotsk
Sakhalin
Kuril Is.
Hokkaido

Mediterranean Sea
Sicily
Caspian Sea
Zagros Mts.
Tien Shan
Pamirs
Kunlun Mts.
Plateau of Tibet
Huang He
North China Plain
Yellow Sea
Sea of Japan
Honshu
Kyushu

hara
aggar Mts.
Tibesti Mts.
Nile River
Red Sea
Plateau of Iran
Himalayas
Ganges
Mt. Everest 8850 m
Yunnan Plateau
Nan Range
East China Sea
Ryukyu Is.
Taiwan
PACIFIC
30°N
TROPIC OF CANCER

hel
Arabian Peninsula
Arabian Sea
Deccan Plateau
Bay of Bengal
Indochina
South China Sea
Philippine Sea
Philippine Is.
Mariana Is.
Guam
OCEAN

Ethiopian Highlands
L. Victoria
Sri Lanka
Maldives
Caroline Is.

Congo R.
Congo Basin
Mt. Kilimanjaro 5895 m
Zanzibar I.
Seychelles
Chagos Archipelago
Sumatra
Borneo
Celebes Sea
Sulawesi
New Guinea
Solomon Is.
EQUATOR   0°

Bie Plateau
Comoros
Java
Timor
Arafura Sea

INDIAN
Madagascar
Mozambique Channel
Mauritius
Great Sandy Desert
Coral Sea
New Caledonia
Fiji Is.

Kalahari Desert
Drakensberg
TROPIC OF CAPRICORN
Mt. Kosciuszko 2228 m
Great Dividing Range
Darling R.
Tasman Sea
North I.
30°S

f Good Hope
OCEAN
Amsterdam I.
St. Paul I.
C. Leeuwin
Bass Strait
Tasmania
South I.

Crozet Is.
Kerguelen I.
180°

60°S

LE
150°E   60°S

NTARCTICA

30°E   60°E   90°E   120°E

ARCTIC   OCEAN
NORTH AMERICA
EUROPE
ASIA
ATLANTIC
AFRICA
PACIFIC
OCEAN
PACIFIC
OCEAN
SOUTH AMERICA
OCEAN
INDIAN
OCEAN
AUSTRALIA
ANTARCTICA

Reference Map

ARCTIC OCEAN

Chukchi Sea *Beaufort Sea* *Baffin Bay* Greenland (Kalaallit Nunaat) (Denmark) *Denmark Strait*

RUSSIA *Bering Strait* *Yukon* Alaska (U.S.) ARCTIC CIRCLE Reykjavik ✪ ICELAND

Anchorage *Bering Sea* *Gulf of Alaska* CANADA *Hudson Bay* *Hudson Str.* *Davis Strait* IRELAND UNITED KI...

60°N *Aleutian Is.* Vancouver Winnipeg *L. Winnipeg* *St. Lawrence R.* Lo...

Seattle *Missouri* *Great Lakes* Montreal Madri...

Chicago Toronto PORTUGAL

UNITED STATES New York City *Azores* (Port.) Casablanca

30°N Los Angeles *Colorado R.* *Mississippi R.* Washington, D.C. *Canary Is.* (Sp.) MORO...

Houston Miami ATLANTIC Western Sahara (adm. Morocco)

TROPIC OF CANCER *Gulf of Mexico* BAHAMAS MAURITANIA

Hawaii (U.S.) PACIFIC MEXICO CUBA HAITI CAPE VERDE SENEGAL

Mexico City ✪ DOM. REP. *Puerto Rico* (U.S.) GAMBIA

BELIZE JAMAICA *Caribbean Sea* DOMINICA GUINEA-BISSAU GUIN...

GUATEMALA HONDURAS BARBADOS SIERRA LEONE C...

EL SALVADOR NICARAGUA TRINIDAD & TOBAGO LIBERIA

COSTA RICA VENEZUELA GUYANA

PANAMA SURINAME

N Bogota French Guiana (Fr.)

EQUATOR COLOMBIA EQUATOR

Galapagos Is. (Ecuador) ECUADOR *Amazon R.* OCEAN

OCEAN PERU BRAZIL

SAMOA *Am. Samoa* (U.S.) Lima ✪ Brasília

TONGA BOLIVIA

Tahiti (Fr.) PARAGUAY Rio de Janeiro

TROPIC OF CAPRICORN Sao Paulo

Easter I. (Chile)

30°S

URUGUAY

Santiago Buenos Aires

CHILE ARGENTINA

Falkland Is. (U.K.)

South Georgia (U.K.)

60°S

ANTARC...

Weddell Sea

INTERNATIONAL DATE LINE

Political Map
WORLD

○○○○○○○○○○○	Continental boundary
▬▬▬▬▬	International boundary
✪ Cairo	National capital
● Shanghai	Major city

Equatorial Scale

```
0        1000        2000 miles
0     1000     2000 kilometers
```

ARCTIC OCEAN

Svalbard (Nor.)

Barents Sea

Kara Sea

New Siberian Is.

East Siberian Sea

ARCTIC CIRCLE

RUSSIA

St. Petersburg

Moscow

Omsk

Novosibirsk

Irkutsk

Sea of Okhotsk

Volga R.

Ob R.

Yenisey R.

Lena R.

Amur R.

60°N

KAZAKHSTAN

Aral Sea

L. Balkhash

Almaty

MONGOLIA

Vladivostok

NORWAY SWEDEN FINLAND

EST. LAT. LITH. BELARUS

GERMANY POLAND

CZ. UKRAINE

AUS. HUNG. MOL.

CRO. BOS. ROMANIA

ITALY SLOV. BULG.

ALB. MAC. YUGO.

GREECE GEORGIA

Rome

Istanbul

TURKEY

ARMENIA

AZERBAIJAN

Black Sea

Caspian Sea

UZBEKISTAN

TURKMENISTAN

KYRGYZSTAN

TAJIKISTAN

Beijing

Huang He

CHINA

NORTH KOREA

SOUTH KOREA

JAPAN

Tokyo

Shanghai

Yellow Sea

PACIFIC

30°N

CYPRUS SYRIA

LEBANON

ISRAEL

JORDAN

IRAQ

Tehran

IRAN

Kabul

AFGHANISTAN

PAKISTAN

Delhi

Ganges R.

NEPAL

BHUTAN

BANGLADESH

Guangzhou

Taipei

TAIWAN

TROPIC OF CANCER

OCEAN

Mediterranean Sea

TUNISIA

Cairo

EGYPT

LIBYA

Riyadh

SAUDI ARABIA

KUWAIT

BAHRAIN QATAR

U.A.E

OMAN

Red Sea

Niger R.

Karachi

Bombay (Mumbai)

INDIA

Calcutta (Kolkata)

MYANMAR (BURMA)

LAOS

South VIETNAM

PHILIPPINES

Manila

Philippine Sea

Northern Mariana Islands (U.S.)

Guam (U.S.)

NIGER

CHAD

SUDAN

ERITREA

YEMEN

DJIBOUTI

ETHIOPIA

SOMALIA

Arabian Sea

Bay of Bengal

THAILAND

Bangkok

CAMBODIA

South China Sea

BRUNEI

FEDERATED STATES OF MICRONESIA

PALAU

NIGERIA

Lagos

CAMEROON

C. AFR. REP.

Congo R.

UGANDA

KENYA

RWANDA

BURUNDI

L. Victoria

SRI LANKA

MALDIVES

MALAYSIA

Singapore

Celebes Sea

EQUATOR

0°

SÃO TOME PRINCIPE

GABON

CONGO REP.

CONGO (ZAIRE)

Kinshasa

Cabinda (Ang.)

Nairobi

TANZANIA

SEYCHELLES

INDONESIA

Jakarta

East Timor (adm. UN)

PAPUA NEW GUINEA

SOLOMON IS.

ANGOLA

ZAMBIA

MALAWI

COMOROS

INDIAN

Arafura Sea

Darwin

VANUATU

FIJI

NAMIBIA

ZIMBABWE

BOTSWANA

MOZAMBIQUE

Mozambique Channel

MADAGASCAR

MAURITIUS

TROPIC OF CAPRICORN

Coral Sea

New Caledonia (Fr.)

30°S

SWAZILAND

SOUTH AFRICA

LESOTHO

Cape Town

OCEAN

Perth

AUSTRALIA

Darling R.

Sydney

Auckland

Melbourne

Bass Strait

Tasman Sea

Wellington

NEW ZEALAND

Kerguelen I. (Fr.)

150°E

60°S

ANTARCTICA

30°E

60°E

90°E

120°E

ARCTIC OCEAN

NORTH AMERICA

EUROPE

ASIA

ATLANTIC

PACIFIC OCEAN

AFRICA

PACIFIC OCEAN

OCEAN

SOUTH AMERICA

INDIAN OCEAN

AUSTRALIA

ANTARCTICA

INTERNATIONAL DATE LINE

30°E 60°E 90°E 120°E 150°E 180

Glossary

abolition: Overthrow of slavery.

Allies: 1. Countries that fought the Central Powers in World War I. Included France, Russia, the United Kingdom, and the United States. 2. Countries that fought the Axis in World War II. Included the Soviet Union, the United Kingdom, and the United States.

amendment: Change made to a law or bill.

annexation: Being added to a larger or more important place.

assassination: Murder of a political or religious leader.

atomic bomb: Destructive weapon that uses nuclear energy to release huge explosive force and intense heat.

Axis: Countries that fought against the Allies in World War II. Included Germany, Italy, and Japan.

blockade: Means of keeping people and goods from entering or leaving a place or region, often using ships.

boundary: Shared border separating places such as states or countries.

cash crop: Crop grown in large amounts and sold for profit, not for personal use.

Central Powers: Countries that fought the Allies in World War I. Included Germany, Austria-Hungry, and the Ottoman Empire.

colony: Settlement or region usually governed by a distant parent country.

Communism: System of government that includes ownership and control of the property and equipment used for producing food, goods, and services.

Confederacy: The 11 southern states that broke away from the United States in 1861. Also called the Confederate States of America.

constitution: Document stating the powers, duties, and structure of a government.

cotton gin: Machine that separates the seeds from the fiber of harvested cotton.

country: 1. Land with one government. 2. Large region, such as the "Oregon Country."

culture: The beliefs, customs, and practices of a group of people.

desegregation: Ending of the separation of one group from others, usually on the basis of race.

discrimination: Making judgments or focusing on differences, sometimes based on prejudice.

economy: System of making, distributing, and buying goods and services.

empire: Set of nations or territories with a single ruler.

export: Something that is sold to another country or to a customer there.

forestry: Use of forests for products such as lumber, paper, and syrup.

Great Britain: European island where England, Wales, and Scotland are located.

immigrant: Person who enters a new country to settle there permanently.

indentured servant: Person who agrees to work for another as payment of a debt or loan.

independence: State of being free from rule by another country.

Indies: European term for the islands and mainland of Southeast Asia, India, and coastal China.

indigo: Plant from which blue dye can be made.

Abbreviations

adm.	administered by	**CO**	Colorado	**Fr.**	France
AK	Alaska	**Congo Rep.**	Congo Republic	**Ft.**	Fort
AL	Alabama	**Cro.**	Croatia	**GA**	Georgia
Alb.	Albania	**CSA**	Confederate States of	**HI**	Hawaii
Am. Samoa	American Samoa		America	**Hung.**	Hungary
Ang.	Angola	**CT**	Connecticut	**I. or Is.**	Island or Islands
Apr.	April	**Cz.**	Czech Republic or	**IA**	Iowa
AR	Arkansas		Czechoslovakia	**ID**	Idaho
Aug.	August	**D.C.**	District of Columbia	**IL**	Illinois
Aus.	Austria	**DE**	Delaware	**IN**	Indiana
AZ	Arizona	**Dec.**	December	**It.**	Italy
Bel.	Belgium	**Den.**	Denmark	**KS**	Kansas
Bos.	Bosnia and Herzegovina	**DMZ**	Demilitarized Zone	**KY**	Kentucky
Br.	Britain	**Dom. Rep.**	Dominican Republic	**L.**	Lake
Bulg.	Bulgaria	**E**	East	**LA**	Louisiana
C.	Cape	**Eq. Guinea**	Equatorial Guinea	**Lat.**	Latvia
CA	California	**Est.**	Estonia	**Lith.**	Lithuania
C. Afr. Rep.	Central African Republic	**FL**	Florida	**Lux.**	Luxembourg